IN THE WORDS OF

FREDERICK
DOUGLASS

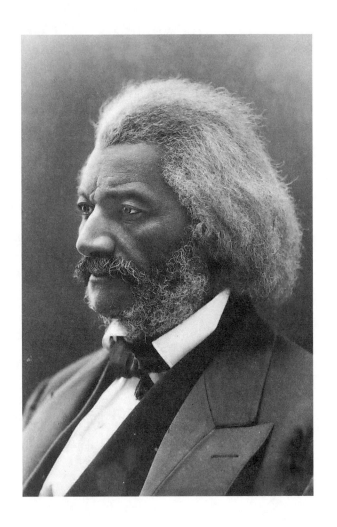

IN THE WORDS OF

FREDERICK DOUGLASS

Quotations from Liberty's Champion

EDITED BY JOHN R. McKIVIGAN
AND HEATHER L. KAUFMAN

FOREWORD BY JOHN STAUFFER

CORNELL UNIVERSITY PRESS
ITHACA AND LONDON

Frontispiece: Frederick Douglass, ca. 1880. From the Collection of the
Rochester Public Library Local History Division.

First published 2012 by Cornell University Press

Printed in the United States of America

Library of Congress Cataloging-in-Publication Data

Douglass, Frederick, 1818–1895.
   In the words of Frederick Douglass : quotations from liberty's
champion / edited by John R. McKivigan and Heather L. Kaufman ;
foreword by John Stauffer.
      p. cm.
   Includes bibliographical references and index.
   ISBN 978-0-8014-4790-7 (cloth : alk. paper)
1. Douglass, Frederick, 1818–1895—Quotations.   2. Douglass,
Frederick, 1818–1895—Political and social views.   3. African
Americans—Civil rights—History—19th century—Quotations,
maxims, etc.   I. McKivigan, John R., 1949–   II. Kaufman,
Heather L., 1969–   III. Title.
   E449.D75A25 2012
   973.8092—dc23
   [B]   2011027254

Cornell University Press strives to use environmentally responsible suppliers
and materials to the fullest extent possible in the publishing of its books. Such
materials include vegetable-based, low-VOC inks and acid-free papers that
are recycled, totally chlorine-free, or partly composed of nonwood fibers. For
further information, visit our website at www.cornellpress.cornell.edu.

Cloth printing   10   9   8   7   6   5   4   3   2   1

For Charles Ambrose Kaufman-McKivigan
whose birth coincided with the final production of
In the Words of Frederick Douglass and whose presence
will be forever imprinted upon its pages.

CONTENTS

CONTENTS

CONTENTS

FOREWORD

The canonization of Frederick Douglass is a relatively new phenomenon. Most Americans today under the age of thirty read Douglass in high school or college and they are familiar with his life story and contributions to American culture. By contrast, most white Americans over the age of fifty—including Ivy League graduates—barely know who Douglass is. They have not read him and often confuse his name with Stephen Douglas, the Illinois senator best remembered for his debates with Abraham Lincoln.

This ignorance among older Americans is striking given Douglass's popularity in the nineteenth century. Following the extraordinary success of his best-selling autobiography, *Narrative of the Life of Frederick Douglass* (1845), he became the most famous black man in the United States, and by the Civil War he was probably the most famous black man in the Western world. He was the first black man to hold a federal appointment that required Senate approval, and he was the nation's first black minister (or ambassador) to Haiti. For most of his adult life he was a household name in the United States and the British Isles, considered one of the nation's preeminent orators and writers, even by those who disagreed with him. And yet for most of the twentieth century his autobiographies were out of print, and few Americans knew who he was or what he had accomplished.

This silencing of Douglass in the twentieth century paralleled the collective amnesia regarding slavery as the fundamental cause of the Civil War. During the sectional and secession crises, no one questioned the centrality of slavery as the wedge that was forcing the nation apart. Every seceding state justified its actions by saying it sought to defend and perpetuate slavery. Mississippi's Declaration of Secession was representative: "Our position is thoroughly identified with the institution of slavery—the greatest material interest in the world."[1] But twenty-five years later, as white Southerners created a new order of black unfreedom, the centrality of slavery in American culture was erased from American memory. Jefferson Davis exemplified this historical revisionism. A leading champion of slavery and its expansion, his proslavery writings greatly contributed to secession and the creation of the Confederacy. But in 1881 he published an influential history of the Civil War, in which he declared that "to whatever extent the question of slavery may have served as an *occasion*, it was far from being the *cause* of the conflict."[2] By keeping blacks unfree until the Civil Rights era of the 1960s, Southerners in effect won the war. And for over a century they controlled how the story of the Civil War got told. Even today, according to Harris interactive polling, a majority of Americans, including two-thirds of white respondents in the former Confederate States, believe that "states rights" rather than slavery was the central cause of the war.[3]

The recent canonization of Douglass thus reflects a larger cultural shift in how Americans remember and understand their past. Thirty years ago, most U.S. history surveys—indeed most books on American history—rarely mentioned blacks, even if they discussed slavery. And most American literature courses focused solely on white authors. The debate over the "canon"—what to include and what to leave out in humanities curricula—became an important battleground in the "culture wars" that reached a boiling point in the 1990s. Both sides understood the implications. Newt Gingrich framed the culture war in terms of another civil war: "the left at its core understands in a way Grant understood after Shiloh that this is a civil war, that only one side will prevail, and the other side will be relegated to history," he said in a 1988 speech. He then sketched out the terms of the fight: "This war has to be fought with the scale and duration and savagery that is only true of civil wars." Gingrich recognized what George Orwell said in 1949 about the power of history: "who controls the past controls the future," and "who controls the present controls the past."[4]

You might call John McKivigan and Heather Kaufman the Grant and Sherman of our cultural civil war. Through their scholarship, especially their work at The Frederick Douglass Papers, they have ensured that Douglass is widely read and will remain a vital force in American culture. They understand his significance: as they point out in their preface, Douglass "stood for what was best in American ideals"—equality before the law for all persons, education, and self-help—and he sought to realize these ideals. Indeed, it's not too much to suggest that if every American were required to read Frederick Douglass, the United States would become a much different—and my view better—place to live.

The current regard for Douglass's insights and wisdom is, of course, not without historical precedent. Lincoln met with Douglass three times at the White House and had immense respect for him. After their first meeting in 1863 he referred to Douglass as "one of the most meritorious men, if not the most meritorious man, in the United States."[5] And at their third meeting, following the Second Inaugural, Lincoln called out to Douglass amid a crowd of whites: "Here comes my friend." He took Douglass by the hand and said,

"I am glad to see you. I saw you in the crowd today, listening to my inaugural address." He asked Douglass how he liked it, adding, "there is no man in the country whose opinion I value more than yours."[6]

Lincoln is not the only president who valued Douglass's opinion. Douglass met with and advised Presidents Johnson, Grant, Hayes, Garfield, Cleveland, and Harrison. More recently President Obama acknowledged Douglass's influence: "The hard, cold facts remind me that it was ... men like Frederick Douglass ... who recognized [that] power would concede nothing without a fight."[7]

Douglass's words continue to serve as inspiration. Indeed they can inspire us, as readers and citizens, to bind up the nation's wounds, complete the unfinished work, and finally fulfill the ideals of freedom and equality of opportunity for all Americans. Collecting Douglass's most powerful and penetrating words, as McKivigan and Kaufman have done, is thus not only an important contribution to history and literature but to the nation.

This book brilliantly highlights the power of Douglass's words. Having exhaustively mined his writings, McKivigan and Kaufman have extracted a mother lode of gold nuggets and organized them topically. The result is truly stunning. While most books of quotations are meant to be sampled, *In the Words of Frederick Douglass* is so well organized, the quotations so penetrating in their critique of nineteenth-century America and yet so resonant with our own time, that you cannot help but get swept up in the beauty of the prose and the narrative threads that McKivigan and Kaufman have woven, and find yourself immersed, reading it as a book rather than an anthology. It will inspire you to read or reread Douglass's autobiographies, speeches, essays, and letters.

JOHN STAUFFER

Notes

1. "A Declaration of the Immediate Causes which Induce and Justify the Secession of the State of Mississippi from the Federal Union," *Journal of the State Convention* (Jackson, MS: E. Barksdale, State Printer, 1861), 86–88.

2. Jefferson Davis, *The Rise and Fall of the Confederate Government*, vol. I (New York; D. Appleton and Company, 1881), 78. See also David W. Blight, *Race and Reunion: The Civil War in American Memory* (Cambridge, Mass.: Harvard University Press, 2001), 258–260.

3. David Von Drehle, "The Civil War, 1861–2011," *Time Magazine*, April 18, 2011, 40–51; David W. Blight, *Race and Reunion: The Civil War in American Memory* (Cambridge, Mass.: Harvard University Press, 2001), 1–30, 381–398.

4. Newt Gingrich, quoted from David Brock, *Blinded by the Right: The Conscience of an Ex-Conservative* (2002; reprint, New York: Three Rivers Press, 2003), 51; George Orwell, *Nineteen Eighty-Four* (1949; reprint, New York: Plume, 2003), 35–36.

5. John Eaton, quoted from *In Memorium: Frederick Douglass* (1897; reprint, Freeport, N.Y.: Books for Libraries, 1971), 71. In an 1864 meeting, Lincoln told Eaton about his first meeting with Douglass a year earlier. See Eaton, *Grant, Lincoln, and the Freedmen* (New York: Longmans, Green, and Co., 1907), 176; John Stauffer, *GIANTS: The Parallel Lives of Frederick Douglass and Abraham Lincoln* (New York: Twelve, 2008), 24, 284.

6. Frederick Douglass, *Life and Times of Frederick Douglass* (1892; reprint, New York: Collier Books, 1962), 366.

7. Barack Obama, *The Audacity of Hope: Thoughts on Reclaiming the American Dream* (2006; reprint, New York: Vintage Books, 2008), 116.

PREFACE

Contemporary Americans recognize Frederick Douglass, a runaway Maryland slave, as the most influential black man of the nineteenth century. Beginning his long public career in 1841 as an agent of the Massachusetts Anti-Slavery Society, Douglass subsequently edited four newspapers and championed many reform movements. He was the only man who played a prominent role at the Seneca Falls meeting in 1848, which formally launched the women's rights movement. He was a temperance advocate and opposed capital punishment, lynching, debt peonage, and the convict lease system. A staunch defender of the Liberty and Republican parties, Douglass held several political appointments, frequently corresponded with leading politicians, and advised Presidents Abraham Lincoln, Ulysses S. Grant, Rutherford B. Hayes, James Garfield, and Benjamin Harrison. He met with John Brown before his abortive raid on Harpers Ferry, helped to recruit African American troops during the Civil War, attended most black conventions held between 1840 and 1895, and served as U.S. ambassador to Haiti.

Douglass was not only the leading representative of nineteenth-century blacks; he stood for what was best in American ideals. An advocate of morality, economic accumulation, self-help, and equality, he believed in racial pride, constant agitation against racial discrimination, vocational education for blacks, nonviolent passive resistance, recognition of the separateness of the black "nation within a nation," and integration of blacks into American society. Antedating Booker T. Washington's emphasis on vocational education and economic self-help, W. E. B. DuBois's calls for political protest, and Martin Luther King's nonviolent direct action, Frederick Douglass is an enduring figure in American history. Douglass's importance has been recognized many times: when he died in 1895, five state legislatures adopted resolutions of regret; in 1967, the U.S. Post Office issued a twenty-five-cent stamp to commemorate the 150th anniversary of his birth; and the federal government selected February to observe as Black History Month because that was the month of Frederick Douglass's birth.

Douglass was one of the leading intellects of the era during and immediately following the Civil War, which some historians dub the "Second Founding." Douglass, Abraham Lincoln, Charles Sumner, Thaddeus Stevens, Elizabeth Cady Stanton, and others seized the opportunity caused by the disruption of the war to advocate that the republican principles, on which the nation had been created, be extended to all of its residents. In the spirit of the original founders, this generation of political actors pushed for an expanded definition of citizenship, liberty, and opportunity that would abolish past racial and gender discrimination and fulfill the original promise of the American Revolution. As perhaps the most articulate voice of this generation, Frederick Douglass's words have at least as much relevance to twenty-first-century readers as those of the first generation of American founders.

Frederick Douglass has left one of the most extensive bodies of significant and quotable public statements of any figure in American history. The editors have compiled nearly seven hundred quotations by Douglass that they judge representative of the breadth and strength of his intellect and interests as well as the eloquence with which he expressed them.

The career of this remarkable African American is amply documented in his autobiographies, speeches, correspondence, and journalistic writings. There are few Americans of any race or profession who left a more extensive written and spoken body of opinions and ideas.

Extraordinarily rare among nineteenth-century Americans, and unique among African Americans, Douglass wrote and published three autobiographies during his lifetime. With each autobiography building on the previous one, Douglass gives his audience an evolving interpretation of the events of his life, offering the reader a different perspective of the man himself. *Narrative of the Life of Frederick Douglass* (1845) and *My Bondage and My Freedom* (1855) show a young, angry, ambitious man at the beginning of his career in the antislavery movement. *Narrative* functioned as propaganda for that movement but also acted as a chilling testimony to the conditions of slavery. *My Bondage and My Freedom* reiterates the horror of slavery but also indicts the *free* states for their racial prejudice and support of slavery. *Life and Times of Frederick Douglass* did not appear until 1881, with an extended version appearing in 1892. Douglass wrote this last memoir to recount his extensive, influential, but lesser-known career following the height of the abolitionist crusade, taking the reader through the tempestuous crisis of the 1850s, the Civil War, and the bureaucracy of the Freedman's Bank; through the vicious political factions of Gilded Age politics; and into Caribbean diplomacy.

Another source of Douglass's ideas and opinions is his journalistic writing. In his lifetime, Douglass owned and operated three weekly newspapers and a monthly magazine. Almost every issue of these publications contained one or more editorials, penned by Douglass, on the pressing issues of his times. In addition to his own journals, Douglass contributed hundreds of columns and essays to the press of his era. Frederick Douglass also was one of the best-known and most highly regarded orators of the nineteenth century. The published reports or manuscript texts for more than 2,500 of Douglass's speeches from the years 1841 to 1895 have survived. In his public speaking, Douglass advocated not just abolition but such other reforms as temperance, public education, and women's rights. For over four decades, he also stumped for numerous political candidates and causes. After the Civil War, Douglass also became a sought-after lyceum lecturer and spoke on varied topics of history, biography, travel, and the arts.

Through a systematic search of manuscript repositories and nineteenth-century newspapers and periodicals, nearly 3,000 letters written by Frederick Douglass have been uncovered. The list of his correspondents reads like a *Who's Who* of the mid- and late-nineteenth century United States and Great Britain. Douglass's correspondence focuses on such varied topics as slavery, abolition, women's rights, temperance, politics, education, economic advancement, international relations, world history, and African American life and culture. Often less-well-known than his published writings, these letters contain Douglass's candid opinions on such topics as slavery, abolition, women's rights, temperance, politics, education, economic advancement, international relations, world history, and African American life and culture.

Given the sheer amount of surviving Douglass documents and the great breadth of topics addressed in them, the editors devoted considerable care to the selection of quotations reproduced in this volume. As interesting and instructive as the details of Douglass's life might be, it was not the editors' intention to create a tool primarily useful for biographical research. Instead, the editors aimed to create a collection of Douglass's quotations that are most revealing about the broader issues of American history as well as inspiring to modern readers seeking wisdom from this iconic figure on modern-day concerns. The editors are confident that the observations, insights, and opinions of Frederick Douglass are still relevant today.

The editors thank Michael McGandy for working diligently with us through all the stages of the editorial process. We are most grateful for his understanding and patience during the last-minute delays in completing the manuscript caused by the early birth of our son Charlie, two weeks before our original deadline.

We also are indebted to John Stauffer of Harvard University, fellow Douglass scholar, for his support of this project and for supplying an insightful foreword.

Finally, we would be shamefully remiss if we failed to thank our past and current colleagues at the Douglass Papers for their labors in providing Frederick Douglass a historical record the equal to that of any other prominent American leader. We hope that this volume will guide many readers to that more substantial body of work.

JOHN R. MCKIVIGAN
HEATHER L. KAUFMAN

IN THE WORDS OF

FREDERICK
DOUGLASS

INTRODUCTION

A Life of Reform

In March 1895, the twenty-seven year-old, newly appointed professor at Wilberforce College in Ohio, W. E. B. DuBois, was invited to address a campus service commemorating the recent death of Frederick Douglass. DuBois had heard Douglass speak only once, but like most African Americans of his generation, he was very familiar with his exploits. He eulogized Douglass as a true statesman, "a man who being in a position to lead, leads." DuBois singled out Douglass's accomplishments: a powerful voice for the abolition of slavery, a successful lobbyist for the enlistment of black soldiers in the Civil War, and an uncompromising champion of the enfranchisement and equal rights of the freedmen. DuBois then attempted to define the lessons of that career for future generations: "As an advocate of civil rights Frederick Douglass stood outside mere race lines and placed himself upon the broad basis of humanity. . . . In this stand the best thought of the 19th century in all the world is with us; and as long as we keep to this broad principle—as long as we condemn lynching men, & not merely condemn lynching Negroes, so long shall we continue slowly but surely to approach the goal which this our Moses placed before us."[1]

Another rising black leader, Booker T. Washington, also attempted to define the lessons of Douglass's life for African Americans born after emancipation: "What he himself was, he had gained by hard work, consecration, temperate habits, and God-fearing conduct toward all of his fellows. . . . Mr. Douglass had richly earned everything that he had, and those who took him as a model were made to realize that success does not come as a gift, but must be deserved and won as a reward for right thinking and high living." For Washington, Douglass was the personification of his own ideology that personal improvement rather than political engagement was the best means for young blacks to advance.[2]

The differing emphases of DuBois's and Washington's interpretations of Douglass's historical significance persisted throughout the next century. During the modern civil rights era, a rancorous debate occurred about the relevance of Douglass's example for solving the racial problems of the nation. He was touted as a champion of nonviolent as well as militant protest by such competing spokespersons for the 1960s civil rights movement as James Foreman, Stokely Carmichael, and Angela Davis. Although for decades Douglass had been held up as a symbol of race pride, many black nationalists of that decade faulted his dedication to integration and other radicals branded his faith in individual economic achievement as naive.[3] Malcolm X combined both critiques and, while conceding Douglass's greatness, advised that black children would be better off being taught about leaders such as Toussaint L'Ouverture, the Haitian revolutionary, "who fought, who bled for freedom, and made others bleed."[4]

In this new century, Douglass remains an enduring political and cultural symbol, but like some other figures of times long passed such as Abraham Lincoln, Thomas Jefferson, George Washington, Susan B. Anthony, John Brown, or even Robert E. Lee, a separation seems to grow inevitably between the iconic figure and his or her actual historical record.[5] With an individual such as Douglass who left a vast amount of public pronouncements, including speeches, editorials, correspondence, and three autobiographies, it seems possible to selectively quote him in support of dozens of contradictory positions. Therefore a brief examination of Douglass's life will be useful to demonstrate that he was a serious thinker, deeply engaged in both the political debates and intellectual currents of his time. Although DuBois's Douglass did "lead," he also observed, analyzed, reflected, and reconsidered his views on multiple issues throughout the nineteenth century. To fully understand Douglass's public statements, it is essential that they be placed within the context his remarkable life story.

Slave Child

Thanks largely to his own autobiographical writings and the dedicated work of his biographers, the details of Frederick Douglass's life are better known than those of any other nineteenth-century African American. He was born on a tobacco plantation on the eastern shore of Maryland and given the name Frederick Augustus Washington Bailey. His mother Harriet was a slave, but his grandmother Betsy Bailey raised him. Soon after Douglass's birth, Harriet was hired out to work on another farm, and she could visit her son only infrequently. Her mother Betsy Bailey was a strong woman, proud of a lineage that she could trace back several generations to a slave "Baly," imported from the West Indies but perhaps born in Africa. In her remote cabin, she raised her grandson until the age of six, when she delivered him to the Wye House plantation, the ancestral base of the powerful Lloyd family. Without advanced warning, Betsy left young Frederick at Wye House and never saw him again as a child, thus ending, according to Nathan I. Huggins, Douglass biographer, "his only real attachment to family."[6]

3

Wye House—Entrance Front. Z24.565VF. Courtesy of the Maryland Historical Society.

Douglass's owner was Aaron Anthony, the Lloyd's principal overseer. Anthony, who some believed was his father, put the boy to work assisting his cook. While still a child, Douglass, hiding in a closet, witnessed Anthony sadistically whip his aunt Hester. He later graphically recounted this and many other inhumane attacks as regular features of slave life on the Lloyd plantation. In contrast, Anthony often indulged young Douglass and allowed him to serve as a companion of one of the Lloyd's male children. The two roamed the forests and swamps, with the young Lloyd shooting game and Douglass retrieving it. Through his contact with the Lloyds, Douglass had a glimpse of an affluent lifestyle far beyond the imaginings of most slaves. As a boy, he sat on the banks of the Chesapeake Bay and dreamed of a better life while watching ships sail by on their way to the far corners of the world. In later antislavery speeches and in his autobiographies, Douglass often recounted details of these early experiences. Not only did he describe his own treatment in order to condemn the inherent inhumanity of the institution of slavery, but he also extolled the importance of family relationships that he had known briefly, if at all.

A significant turning point in Douglass's life came in 1826 when Anthony "loaned" the young slave to his daughter's brother-in-law, Hugh Auld. Auld was a Baltimore shipwright who wanted the young slave as companion for his own son, "Tommy," and as a helper around the house for his wife, Sophia Auld, who had never before had a slave under her control. According to Dickson Preston, Douglass biographer, "she could no more treat him as an inferior than one of her own children."[7] Sophia Auld even began to teach the black youth to read. When her husband discovered this, he ordered these lessons ended, declaring, as Douglass recalled, "learning would do him no good, but probably, a great deal of harm—making him disconsolate and unhappy. If you learn him now to read, he'll want to know how to write; and, this accomplished, he'll be running away with himself."[8] If anything, Auld's opposition encouraged Douglass to become literate. He bribed local school children with sweets stolen from the Auld's kitchen to continue his education until he had mastered reading.

At some point in his Baltimore youth, Douglass acquired a copy of Caleb Bingham's textbook on English grammar and rhetoric, the *Columbia Orator*, first published in 1797. This work contained excerpts from speeches by such famous orators as Cicero, William Pitt, and Charles James Fox. Not only did these men's words serve as models that inspired the young Douglass to enter public life, but also an essay on oratorical skills added by Bingham influenced his later speaking style. William McFeely, Douglass biographer, has observed that Douglass took to heart Bingham's analysis of Cicero: "The best judges of the ancients have represented Pronunciation, which they likewise called Action, as the principal part of an orator's province." According to McFeely, Douglass thereafter believed that if "he could say words—say them correctly, say them beautifully, [he] could act; he could matter in the world."[9] Much of the striving for eloquent expression that marked Douglass's speeches can be traced to his absorption of Bingham's lessons.

By 1833, Aaron Anthony had died and Douglass became the property of Anthony's son-in-law, Thomas Auld, a storekeeper in the small village of St. Michaels, back on the Maryland eastern shore. After a quarrel between the Auld brothers, Thomas Auld had the fifteen-year-old slave returned to him at St. Michaels. Douglass found the routines of village life boring after having lived in Baltimore. He got into serious trouble for attempting to operate a clandestine Sunday school for local blacks. To instill more discipline in this overindulged slave, Auld "hired out" Douglass to work for a year on the farm of the most notorious "slave breaker" in the area, Edward Covey. Determined to make him a more pliant slave, Covey underfed and overworked the young man. Escalating tensions between the two culminated in a brutal two-hour-long showdown in August 1834 in which Douglass successfully resisted all attempts by Covey to tie and whip him. Douglass later recalled,

> After resisting him [Edward Covey], I felt as I had never felt before. It was a resurrection from the dark and pestiferous tomb of slavery, to the heaven of comparative freedom. I was no longer a servile coward, trembling under the form of a brother worm of the dust, but, my long-cowed spirit was roused to an attitude of manly independence. I had reached the point, at which I was not afraid to die. This spirit made me a freeman in *fact*, while I remained a slave in *form*.[10]

6

Waldo Martin, historian, judges this fight as "the most important event in Douglass's journey from thralldom to liberty. It graphically heralded his lifelong dedication to resistance against oppression."[11] Douglass did not define that "manly independence" in contrast to feminine traits; rather, he identified manhood in terms of freedom contrasted with enslavement. In future years, this identification enabled him to vigorously support the women's rights movement while still behaving as a proper Victorian in his own domestic relations.

The following year, Auld hired out Douglass to work on the farm owned by a less violent master, William Freeland. Although Douglass never complained of his treatment by Freeland, he had grown more desirous than ever of obtaining his freedom. He plotted with four other slaves to steal a small boat and sail North to freedom. A fellow slave probably exposed their conspiracy, and all were arrested and jailed. As the ringleader, Douglass expected to be made an example and "sold South" to the distant cotton fields of Alabama or Mississippi. Instead, Thomas Auld decided to give his slave one last chance and returned him to live with his brother's family in Baltimore. Auld even promised to free Douglass at age twenty-five if he behaved obediently.

Douglass has left eloquent testimony about his treatment as a young slave. He reflected often on the distorted values and behaviors of the slaveholders he had encountered. Although he was not physically abused to the extent that many slaves were, the scenes of brutality the youthful Douglass witnessed allowed him to condemn the system of human bondage as fundamentally antithetical to human rights. His opportunity to become literate in the Auld's Baltimore household instilled in him an appreciation for education and self-improvement that became a lifelong theme in his oratory and writing.[12]

The Runaway Slave

Hugh Auld put the teenage Douglass to work on the Baltimore docks. In time, Douglass acquired valued skills as a ship caulker although he had to endure racially motivated attacks from white coworkers. With his labor rented out to various shipbuilding companies, he generated considerable revenue for Auld. Perhaps to motivate Douglass to work even harder and out of his own arrogance as a slave owner, Auld allowed the slave to seek out his own employers and to live outside the household. Auld's only requirement was that Douglass weekly turn over the bulk of his wages. Douglass later observed, "Master Hugh . . . with this arrangement . . . had armed my love of liberty with a lash and driver, far more efficient than any I had known before known; and, while he derived all the benefits of slaveholding by the arrangement, without its evils, I endured all the evils of being a slave, and yet suffered all the care and anxiety of a responsible freeman."[13]

Free of intensive white supervision, Douglass joined a small black Methodist congregation and mixed socially with the large Baltimore free black community. In 1837 or early 1838, he met Anna Murray, a free black originally from the Eastern Shore who worked as a maid for a wealthy white family. Together, the two planned for a life in freedom. Historians have observed that Douglass's time in Baltimore "had equipped him for a life beyond slavery, providing him with an education and socialization that was a rare privilege for a slave youth."[14]

In September 1838, Douglass escaped from Auld by disguising himself as a free black sailor on shore leave. He boldly took a train to New York City where Anna rendezvoused with him, and the two were married. For greater security, the couple settled in New Bedford, Massachusetts, where they sought anonymity among the large free black population of the city. To make it harder for Auld to discover his new home, he dropped the surname "Bailey." Originally, he had considered adopting the surname "Johnson," but he discovered it was already too common a pseudonym among the large New Bedford population of runaway slaves. Instead, he selected "Douglass," the name of a leading character from Sir Walter Scott's *Lady of the Lake*, on account of its heroic sound. His reading now unfettered, Douglass immersed himself in the novels of Scott, the poetry of Lord Byron and Robert Burns, and the plays of William Shakespeare, all authors from whom he would quote freely in later years.[15]

Although residing in a free state, Douglass encountered considerable racial discrimination when he sought work in New Bedford. He had to work as a day laborer on the docks rather than a caulker due to the opposition of white artisans. He later recalled that "It was new, dirty, and hard work for me; but I went at it with a glad heart and a willing hand. I was now my own master. It was a happy moment, the rapture of which can be understood only by those who have been slaves."[16] Douglass and his wife also derived great pleasure from joining the African Methodist Episcopal Zion Church. Douglass became a lay preacher, and the experience as a public speaker that he gained in the church proved invaluable in his later career. In many later public speeches, he applied the biblical and other religious imagery he learned during these years to his commentary on contemporary political events.

By the time Douglass had reached the North in the later 1830s, a small but vocal campaign was underway to abolish slavery. Resistance to slavery, of course, had begun practically with the establishment of human bondage in the Americas. Slave rebels were certainly the first abolitionists and inspired others to join in the emancipation crusade. The small but growing communities of free African Americans also denounced the enslavement of their brethren. In the 1820s, most free black leaders had rallied against the efforts of the American Colonization Society to persuade them to abandon the United States for a new home in Africa.[17] The testimony of these African Americans, plus the success of the campaign by British evangelicals against slavery in the British Caribbean colonies, motivated some American whites to also began to speak out against the physical and moral mistreatment of the slaves. Aided by the religious fervor of the recent Second Great Awakening, the American movement for immediate abolition had grown rapidly despite encountering major opposition from the leading U.S. political and religious institutions. In 1840, the still young abolitionist movement splintered into a number of competing factions over issues of the most effective tactics to pursue. Some favored working through the churches and others through governmental institutions to abolish slavery.[18]

In New England, in particular, many abolitionists followed the leadership of William Lloyd Garrison, a white journalist. These Garrisonians favored a coalition of abolitionists with other reformers pursuing such goals as women's rights, temperance, and pacifism. Only a year out of Maryland slavery, Douglass began a subscription to Garrison's weekly Boston newspaper, *The Liberator.* Douglass later reported that he found that the "Liberator was a paper after my own heart. It detested slavery—exposed hypocrisy and wickedness in high places—made no truce with the traffickers in the bodies and souls of men; it preached human brotherhood, denounced oppression, and, with all the solemnity of God's word, demanded the complete emancipation of my race."[19] It was through reading the *Liberator* articles written by well-educated Garrisonian men and women that Douglass greatly expanded his knowledge of mid-nineteenth-century political and intellectual currents as well as the specific issues related to ongoing reform campaigns.[20]

Douglass attended some abolitionist meetings in New Bedford and heard Garrison lecture. Impressed by the abolitionist's commitment to black rights, Douglass attended a regional abolitionist convention

"I am in earnest. I will not equivocate—I will not excuse—I will not retreat a single inch—AND I WILL BE HEARD."

Wm Lloyd Garrison

William Lloyd Garrison (1805–1879). After daguerreotype by Lorenzo G. Chase. National Portrait Gallery, Smithsonian Institution/Art Resource, N.Y.

on the island of Nantucket in August 1841. Inspired to speak, he briefly told the audience some of his own experiences as a slave. His novice performance convinced the Garrisonians to recruit Douglass to become one of their traveling lecturers. Initially, he described only his personal experiences to curious Northern audiences, always remaining careful not to disclose details that would reveal his true identify. In a short time, however, Douglass mastered the abolitionists' full arsenal of arguments against slavery in his speeches. His orations became so erudite that critics of the abolitionists charged that Douglass could never have been born a slave as he claimed.[21] To defend his credibility, Douglass in 1845 published the first of his three autobiographies, *Narrative of the Life of Frederick Douglass,* which provided all of the specific details of his birth, ownership, and life in Maryland. However, to protect fugitive slaves from capture by their Southern masters, Douglass did not include details of his escape from slavery.

Contemporaries as well as modern-day scholars regard Douglass's *Narrative* as one of the greatest literary works produced by the American antislavery crusade. *Narrative* has been quoted repeatedly, first by other abolitionists and subsequently by historians and literary scholars, for its insights on the damaging impact of slavery on both the bondsman and the master. One Irish reviewer called *Narrative* "a literary wonder. The incidents of his life are such a kind as to hold the reader spellbound, while they are related in a style simple, perspicuous, and eloquent."[22] Widely accepted today as the epitome of the fugitive slave narrative genre, Douglass's first autobiography is perhaps the most studied work of African American literature of all times.[23]

Abolitionist Hero

His identity as a fugitive slave now public, Douglass's friends warned him that his recapture and return to slavery was a real possibility. For his personal safety, Douglass fled to Great Britain. For nearly two years, he toured the British Isles lecturing on behalf of the abolitionist cause. He traveled through Ireland and observed the famine. After also witnessing there the evils of heavy drinking, Douglass was converted to the cause of temperance. For the next half century Douglass lectured to audiences about the deleterious consequences of alcohol consumption, branding intemperance "the parent of wretchedness, want and idleness. . . ."[24] In Scotland, he created considerable controversy by his vehement attacks on clergy there who had solicited contributions from American slaveholders. The support that many American denominations lent to slavery by accepting slave owners into their membership caused Douglass to scold religious institutions for compromising fundamental moral principles. He told an Irish audience that he "loved and cherished the sacred principles of Christianity; but he despised the man-trapping, woman-whipping, slave-branding and cradle-robbing Christianity of America. . . ."[25] Like many of his Garrisonian colleagues, he adopted a jeremiad stance in his public pronouncements, which lamented the low state that slavery had taken American morality, and prophesized divine retribution unless a sweeping reform was undertaken.[26]

Douglass's enthusiastic reception in Great Britain greatly elevated his self-confidence. He was welcomed into the homes of middle-class reformers as well as the manors of titled nobility and observed the absence of racism exhibited by his hosts. Douglass's abolitionist rhetoric thereafter denounced the hypocrisy of the democratic pretensions of his own republic compared to the civility found in the British monarchy. He spoke repeatedly on this theme over the next three decades as a principal orator at annual celebrations sponsored by African Americans to honor the British emancipation of slaves in the West Indies in the 1830s.[27] In late 1846, English abolitionist sympathizers purchased his freedom from Auld and gave Douglass funds to return to the United States and start his own newspaper. Douglass left Britain, according to one study of that trip, "the finished independent man, cut from a whole cloth and able to make his own decisions about the strategies and ideologies of the abolitionist movement."[28]

The founding of the *North Star* (later the *Frederick Douglass' Paper*) in Rochester, New York, in late 1847 marked the beginning of Douglass's personal political ideology. In his first years as an abolitionist, Douglass espoused the Garrisonian tenets that the Constitution was a proslavery document and eschewed voting as an act that endorsed a government that protected slavery. He condemned not only the two major political parties of the era, the Whigs and the Democrats, but also the small Liberty Party founded by abolitionist opponents of Garrison in 1840.[29] Douglass's speeches and *North Star* editorials attacked not just slavery and the racism found in Northern society but also offered incisive commentary on a wide range of contemporary social trends and cultural developments.

PROSPECTUS
FOR AN ANTI-SLAVERY PAPER, TO BE ENTITLED
NORTH STAR.

FREDERICK DOUGLASS

Proposes to publish, in ROCHESTER, N. Y., a **WEEKLY ANTI-SLAVERY PAPER**, with the above title.

The object of the NORTH STAR will be to attack SLAVERY in all its forms and aspects; advocate UNIVERSAL EMANCIPATION; exalt the standard of PUBLIC MORALITY; promote the Moral and Intellectual Improvement of the COLORED PEOPLE; and hasten the day of FREEDOM to the Three Millions of our ENSLAVED FELLOW COUNTRYMEN.

The Paper will be printed upon a double medium sheet, at $2,00 per annum, if paid in advance, or $2,50, if payment be delayed over six months.

The names of Subscribers may be sent to the following named persons, and should be forwarded, as far as practicable, by the first of November, proximo.

FREDERICK DOUGLASS, Lynn, Mass.
SAMUEL BROOKE, Salem, Ohio.
M. R. DELANY, Pittsburgh, Pa.
VALENTINE NICHOLSON, Harveysburgh, Warren Co. O.
Mr. WALCOTT, 21 Cornhill, Boston.

JOEL P. DAVIS, Economy, Wayne County, Ind.
CHRISTIAN DONALDSON, Cincinnati, Ohio.
J. M. MKIM, Philadelphia, Pa.
AMARANCY PAINE, Providence, R. I.
Mr. GAY, 142 Nassau Street, New York.

SUBSCRIBERS' NAMES.		RESIDENCE.		NO. OF COPIES.

Prospectus for an anti-slavery paper to be entitled *North Star*.
Schomburg Center/Art Resource, N.Y.

Even though Douglass's writings at this time generally followed the Garrisonian line, he detected signs that many white Garrisonians disapproved of his more elevated and independent role in the movement as a newspaper editor. Offended by what he viewed as paternalism, Douglass's loyalties began to waiver. In his editorial columns, he questioned the Garrisonian orthodoxy regarding the Constitution and wondered in print whether political means might be effective against slavery. Years later, Douglass reflected on the many intellectual benefits he had derived from taking on the responsibilities of editing his own weekly newspaper: "it was the best school possible for me. It obliged me to think and read, it taught me to express my thoughts clearly, and was perhaps better than any other course I could have adopted. Besides, it made it necessary for me to lean upon myself, and not upon the heads of our Anti-Slavery church, to be a principal, and not an agent."[30] This was the beginning of Douglass's serious study of the government and Constitution of the United States and of the responsibilities of citizenship, all subjects on which he offered many perceptive observations over the years.

Locating operations for the *North Star* in upstate New York, far from the Garrisonian center of strength in New England, Douglass sought out new friends and allies. In 1848, he attended the national convention in Buffalo, New York, that founded the Free Soil Party. Although disappointed that the new party failed to call for the immediate emancipation of the slaves, Douglass gave a qualified endorsement to its platform opposing the extension of slavery into the western territories. Acknowledging the shortcomings in the Free Soilers' positions, Douglass observed aptly that "what is morally right is not always politically possible."[31] In the early 1850s, Douglass came into closer contact with abolitionists in his new home region who supported political antislavery tactics. Their leader, Gerrit Smith, a wealthy landowner, impressed Douglass by his absence of racial condescension.[32] In 1851, Douglass merged his financially struggling newspaper with a Liberty Party periodical underwritten by Smith. The move marked Douglass's final defection from the Garrisonians to the political antislavery camp. Throughout the 1850s, Douglass wavered between support for the anti-extensionist Free Soil Party and its successor, the Republican Party, and Smith's tiny political abolitionist faction, which claimed that the federal government had the constitutional power to abolish slavery.

Douglass's preference for political activism led to his acrimonious expulsion from the Garrisonian abolitionist ranks. There were charges that he had been "bought" by Smith's generous contributions. There were even nastier imputations that Douglass's personal life was out of order. Rumors circulated that Douglass had developed an improper intimacy with his white editorial assistant, Julia Griffiths, who had come from England to help him with the *North Star.* Douglass came to believe that the Garrisonians' anger toward him was largely motivated by their paternalist belief that the former fugitive slave should forever remain indebted to his original white sponsors.

In a thoughtfully prepared address in 1855 to the Rochester Ladies' Anti-Slavery Society, Douglass attempted to step back from the acrimony and offer a balanced assessment of the progress of American abolitionism. He praised Garrison's leading role in organizing the antislavery movement in the early 1830s, but contended that the white abolitionist "neither discovered its principles, originated its ideas, nor framed its arguments. These are all older than the preacher."[33] Douglass traced the origins of antislavery sentiments instead back to early religious preaching, the ideology of the American Revolution, and free black resistance to the colonization movement. He then appraised the strengths and weaknesses displayed by each of the competing abolitionist factions. Conceding the damage caused by factional infighting among abolitionists, Douglass concluded his assessment of the movement on an optimistic beat: "Present organizations may perish—but the cause will go on. That cause has a life, distinct and independent of the organizations patched up from time to time to carry it forward. Looked at apart from the bones and sinews, and body, it is a thing immortal. It is the very essence of justice, Liberty, and love."[34]

Facing difficult financial times with a growing family and the loss of many of his earliest Garrisonian subscribers, Douglass and Griffiths struggled to keep their antislavery newspaper afloat. Douglass traveled widely, lecturing and collecting in new subscriptions. Griffiths edited a series of gift books entitled the *Liberty Bell*, the proceeds from which went to Douglass's newspaper. For the 1853 issue of the *Liberty Bell*, Douglass wrote a novella, "The Heroic Slave," one of the first fictional works by an African American author. This work was a fictionalized defense of an actual shipboard slave uprising led by Madison Washington in 1841.[35]

In 1855, Douglass also published his second autobiography, *My Bondage and My Freedom*. This work carried on the *Narrative*'s assault on the mistreatment of Southern slaves but also added a lengthy indictment of the Northern racial discrimination that Douglass had endured since fleeing Maryland. In comparison to *Narrative*, Douglass in *My Bondage and My Freedom* offers deeper psychological insights into the damaging impact of plantation life on master as well as slave. McFeely observes that readers of this second autobiography "will find a Frederick Douglass of a far more critical and analytical mind than the one in the *Narrative*."[36] Nevertheless, the reading public, then and today, has evinced a preference for the more pristine language of Douglass's first autobiography. Eric Sundquist, literary scholar, argues that, in the later work, Douglass's prose had adopted an almost oratorical character: "It is exactly such language that some modern readers have found regrettable in *My Bondage and My Freedom*. Yet the text

Portrait of Frederick Douglass, abolitionist.
Engraved by J. C. Buttre from a daguerreotype.

Source: "My Bondage and My Freedom" by Frederick Douglass.
New York, Auburn: Miller, Orton & Mulligan, 1855.
Schomburg Center/Art Resource, N.Y.

reminds us often that the language of revolutionary liberation and the language of sentiment are virtually synonymous, not just in the best antislavery writing but in the whole era's grappling with the problem of bondage."[37]

Fighting for Freedom

In the 1850s, Douglass expanded his leadership in the Northern free black community. He resisted segregation policies on ships and railroad cars at the risk of physical injury and withdrew his children from segregated schools in Rochester. Douglass attended major conventions of free blacks and strongly advocated both self-help and civil rights. He helped lead a series of campaigns in New York to win equal voting rights for black men.[38] Douglass also publicly battled with other black leaders such as Martin Delany and Henry Highland Garnet, who advocated emigration back to Africa as the best course for the elevation of their race. For decades to come, Douglass articulated a consistent position in speeches and writings against all efforts to persuade African Americans to depart the United States for a new homeland.[39]

After she published *Uncle Tom's Cabin* in 1852, Douglass befriended Harriet Beecher Stowe. This relationship developed gingerly because Douglass in his *Heroic Slave* had intentionally sought to refute the image of the passive slave embodied by Stowe's Uncle Tom character.[40] As their mutual trust grew, Douglass encouraged Stowe to offer financial support to establish a black manual arts college and abandon her endorsement of colonization schemes.[41]

Also during the 1850s, Douglass was an active conductor on the famous Underground Railroad. He hid runaway slaves in his own house until he was able to assist them to reach Canada, where they would be safe from recapture by their masters. Although he championed the activities of other Underground Rail conductors in his editorials and speeches, he maintained a strict silence about his own part in aiding fugitives until well after the end of slavery. He later explained this secrecy as a tactical calculation: "Such is my detestation of slavery, that I would keep the merciless slaveholder profoundly ignorant of the means of flight adopted by the slave. He should be left to imagine himself surrounded by myriads of invisible tormentors, ever ready to snatch, from his infernal grasp, his trembling prey."[42] While he hid his personal participation in the Underground Railroad, Douglass's speeches and editorial throughout the 1850s loudly denounced the effort by the federal government to capture and return runaway slaves to the South. In 1852, for example, he declared, "In glaring violation of justice, in shameless disregard of the forms of administering law, in cunning arrangement to entrap the defenseless, and in diabolical intent, this Fugitive Slave Law stands alone in the annals of tyrannical legislation."[43]

In the 1850s, Douglass also was drawn deeply into the conspiracy led by John Brown, the white abolitionist. Douglass met Brown while on an abolitionist lecture tour of Massachusetts and was impressed by the latter's freedom from racial prejudices. Brown was searching for more aggressive means of freeing slaves and devised a plot to lead an armed band into the South via the Appalachian Mountains. Hiding in camps deep in those mountains, Brown's followers planned to raid plantations, free slaves, and eventually foment a massive rebellion. In the mid-1850s, Brown with several sons migrated to Kansas Territory and played a well-publicized role in the guerrilla skirmishing between supporters of creating a free state there and settlers wanting a slave state.

In January 1858, Brown visited Rochester and stayed several weeks as a guest in Douglass's home. There Brown sharpened his original plan to invade the South and attempted to recruit Douglass into the conspiracy. With a family of five children to support, Douglass rejected these entreaties but helped Brown to find supporters in both black and white abolitionist circles.[44] As David Blight, historian, observes, Douglass "did not lack physical courage, he was simply too much a realist to join the Harpers Ferry raid. Douglass was also wise enough to know that rhetoric was his best weapon."[45] After Brown's attack failed, authorities uncovered documents linking Douglass to the plot. Fearing arrest, Douglass fled first to Canada and then to Great Britain. Only after the furor died down the following year did Douglass believe it safe to return to Rochester.

For the remainder of his life, Douglass strongly championed the memory of John Brown as a martyr for freedom. He defended Brown's employment of violent means as a justifiable response to the terror employed daily against the slaves. Douglass editorialized, "Slavery is a system of brute force. It shields itself behind might, rather than right. It must be met with its own weapons. Capt. Brown has initiated a new mode of carrying on the crusade of freedom, and his blow has sent dread and terror throughout the entire ranks of the piratical army of slavery."[46] In an 1860 speech Douglass branded slavery as "A standing insurrection from beginning to end—a perpetual chronic insurrection. . . . John Brown merely stepped in to interrupt and arrest this insurrection against the rights and liberties of mankind; and he did right."[47] He also praised Brown's moral courage in challenging enormous odds: "His deeds might be disowned, but the spirit which made those deeds possible was worthy highest honor."[48]

Shortly after Douglass's return from his post–Harpers Ferry exile, the attention of the nation turned to the crisis produced by the election of Republican Party candidate, Abraham Lincoln, to the presidency. Douglass reluctantly endorsed Lincoln but criticized the weakness of the Republican platform, which opposed only the spread of slavery to the western territories.[49] Eleven slaveholding states, however,

John Brown (1800–1859).
Library of Congress.

believed that Lincoln in the White House was a dire threat to the institution of slavery, and they seceded. Soon the nation was plunged into a bloody civil war. Initially in his editorial columns, Douglass was critical of Lincoln for failing to make abolition the war goal of the North. Then, following the president's issuance of the Emancipation Proclamation, Douglass became an energetic supporter of Lincoln and the Union cause. In an important 1864 address entitled "The Mission of the War," Douglass now fully endorsed the war for its goal of emancipation: "The world has witnessed many wars—and history records and perpetuates their memory, but the world has not seen a nobler and grander war than that which the loyal people of this country are now waging against the slaveholding Rebels. The blow we strike is not merely to free a country or continent—but the whole world from Slavery—for when Slavery falls here—it will fall everywhere."[50]

According to Blight, Douglass's "millennialist interpretation of the war caused him caused him to see the conflict as a cleansing tragedy, wherein the nation had been redeemed of its evil by lasting grace."[51]

With the antislavery goal of the war clarified, Douglass crisscrossed the North laboring as a recruiter of black soldiers. Douglass called on his fellow blacks to use military service as a way to dispel Northern white racial prejudices and as a means to lay claim to full citizenship following Union victory. In one 1863 address, he declared, "Once let the black man get upon his person the brass letters U.S. let him get an eagle on his button, and a musket on his soldier, and bullets in his pocket, and there is no power on the earth or under the earth which can deny that he has earned the right of citizenship in the United States. I say again, this is our chance, and woe betide us if we fail to embrace it!"[52]

Two of Douglass's three sons joined black regiments of the Union Army and served with distinction. Douglass personally met three times with President Abraham Lincoln in Washington and advised him on the best ways to employ blacks in the military effort. In later years, Douglass recalled that Lincoln had received him graciously at the White House and listened to his recommendations respectfully. With racism increasing later in the century, Douglass reminisced, "Mr. Lincoln was not only a great President, but a GREAT MAN—too great to be small in anything. In his company, I was never in any way reminded of my humble origin, or of my unpopular color."[53]

Reconstruction

The friendly treatment by Lincoln, coupled with the Republicans' support for the Thirteenth Amendment ending slavery, made Douglass a staunch Republican for the remainder of his life. As John Stauffer, historian, observes, after the war Douglass for the first time in his life was an "insider" who enjoyed exercising influence on national policymaking as the leading spokesperson for his emancipated race.[54] From that vantage point, Douglass shrewdly critiqued the inner workings of the federal government as well as the character of both political parties and their leaders. Early in Reconstruction, Douglass aligned with the Radical Republicans and loudly opposed the conciliatory policies of Lincoln's successor, Andrew Johnson, toward the defeated Confederates.[55] As Johnson permitted Southerners to attempt to return the emancipated African Americans to a slavelike status, Douglass's speeches articulated a trenchant analysis of problems in the federal system and constitutional balance of powers. Douglass proposed a sweeping series of constitutional reforms, not just to ensure equal rights but to enhance the very democratic character of the American government.[56] For example, Douglass condemned the presidential veto, brandished frequently by Johnson to attempt to block legislation to protect the freedmen, as "alien to every idea of republican government—borrowed from the old world, from king craft and priest craft, and all other adverse craft to republican government. It is anti-republican, anti-democratic, anti-common sense."[57]

In 1870, Douglass relocated from Rochester to Washington, D.C., where he assisted two of his sons in editing a weekly political newspaper, the *New National Era.* Once again, his editorial pen expounded the demand for equal treatment of all races by the national government. He briefly headed the Freedman's Savings Bank, but found that institution to be so financially unstable that his efforts could not prevent its closure or the consequent loss of the meager savings of thousands of former slaves.[58]

As a powerful orator with a large following among both African Americans and white abolitionists, Douglass was recruited by the

Residence of Frederick Douglass, Washington, D.C. From the collection
of the Rochester Public Library Local History Division.

Republicans to stump in both presidential and state election campaigns. A loyal party worker and an acknowledged leading black
Republican, Douglass received a number of political appointments
in the postbellum years, including the offices of assistant secretary
to the U.S. Santo Domingo Commission (1871), the U.S. marshal
(1877–1881) and recorder of deeds for the District of Columbia
(1881–1886), and minister resident to the Republic of Haiti
(1889–1891). Booker T. Washington noted that Douglass regarded
these government appointments "to mean some fresh recognition of
the worth of the Negro race."[59]

Another major reason for Douglass's strong partisan loyalties
was the condition of his fellow blacks in the former slave states.
As Reconstruction progressed, resistance grew to Republican attempts to assist freed slaves to attain full citizenship and economic

opportunities. Many Southern whites resisted such efforts politically with membership in the Democratic Party and violently through groups such as the Ku Klux Klan. As Democrats gradually regained control of Southern state governments, Douglass advised blacks to remain loyal to the party of Lincoln because "the Republican party is the deck, all outside is the sea."[60]

Inside the Republican Party, Douglass aligned with the Stalwart faction, believing that white politicians such as Ulysses S. Grant, John A. Logan, and Roscoe Conkling had a stronger record of support for civil rights than competing Republican leaders. Douglass particularly was displeased with the relative indifference that Rutherford B. Hayes, James A. Garfield, and James G. Blaine displayed toward black rights. Nonetheless, Douglass fought against any suggestion that African Americans split their votes between the two major parties to gain more leverage with each. In speeches directed toward white audiences, Douglass strongly counseled against concessions to the growing mood of sectional reconciliation. He reminded Northerners that "there was a right side and a wrong side in the late war, which no sentiment ought to cause us to forget."[61]

Douglass campaigned vigorously on behalf of his race for passage and ratification of two more constitutional amendments, the Fourteenth to recognize black citizenship and the Fifteenth to confer the vote on black males. The latter proposal produced a serious quarrel between black leaders and many proponents of woman suffrage. Women's rights supporters favored an amendment to enfranchise all adults, male and female, black and white. Douglass had steadfastly supported the women's rights campaign since his attendance at the Seneca Falls Convention in 1848, but felt that combining that cause with black male suffrage would probably defeat both at that time. After the successful ratification of the Fifteenth Amendment, he went back to work for woman suffrage and campaigned for that cause up to his death. Over nearly a half century, he left a large body of eloquent pleas for full citizenship for female Americans. For example, Douglass told an 1888 audience that "the government that excludes women from all participation in its creation, administration and perpetuation, maims itself, deprives itself of one-half of all that is wisest and best for its usefulness, success and perfection."[62]

Douglass viewed his support for women's rights partially as repayment for the dedicated effort of many female abolitionists on behalf of the emancipation of his race but also as the fulfillment of a more comprehensive vision of reform; as he declared, "All good causes are mutually helpful. The benefits accruing from this movement for the equal rights of woman are not confined or limited to woman only. They will be shared by every effort to promote the progress and welfare of mankind everywhere and in all ages."[63] Douglass sought to welcome women as the equals of men into the political sphere; however, his view of gender roles inside the household remained a traditional one.

During the post–Civil War decades, Douglass became a sought-after lyceum lecturer. He toured the country to speak on such diverse topics as ethnology, photography, self-made men, and the Protestant Reformation. These addresses provide numerous examples of the wisdom that Douglass had acquired through a lifetime of rigorous self-education. They also provide valuable insight into Douglass's thinking on a considerable range of the intellectual and cultural issues of the last third of the nineteenth century. Douglass confided in the leading U.S. lyceum operator, James Redpath, that his lectures drew large audiences largely because of his fame as a former slave and abolitionist. The lyceum-going public, he reported, "do not attend lectures to hear statesmanlike addresses, which are usually rather heavy for the stomachs of young and old who listen. People want to be amused as well as instructed. They come as often for the former as the latter, and perhaps as often to see the man as for either."[64]

After the Civil War, Douglass frequently used the podium to advise black audiences about the virtues of education, enterprise, and thrift. He exhorted a Virginia audience, "if man is without education although with all his latent possibility attaching to him he is, as I have said, but a pitiable object; a giant in body but a pigmy in intellect, and at best but half a man. Without education he lives within the narrow, dark and grimy walls of ignorance. He is a poor prisoner without hope."[65] As he had argued throughout his public career, African American economic achievement would be a sure answer to white racial prejudice.[66]

In 1879, Douglass became enmeshed in a serious controversy among black leaders when he advised Southern blacks not to migrate to the prairie states but to remain in the South and struggle there for full equality. Black opponents charged that Douglass was losing touch with the grim realities facing most members of his race. In a carefully prepared paper for a meeting of the American Social Science Association, Douglass responded,

> The habit of roaming from place to place in pursuit of better conditions of existence is by no means a good one. A man should never leave his home for a new one till he has earnestly endeavored to make his immediate surroundings accord with his wishes. . . . No people ever did much for themselves or for the world, without the sense and inspiration of native land; of a fixed home; of a familiar neighborhood, and common associations.[67]

Rather than being callous to the suffering of the Southern freedmen, Douglass's position demonstrated a commitment to racial self-improvement and an unabated optimism that American race relations could be improved. From the antebellum colonization movement to

28

the African emigration plans advanced in the 1850s to the Exoduster movement after Reconstruction, Douglass consistently opposed such "Utopian and impossible enterprises" as a diversion from the struggle for racial justice at home.[68]

Douglass also was the center of a second, more personal controversy when, following the death of his wife Anna in 1881, he married

Anna Murray Douglass. Courtesy National Park Service, Museum Management Program and Frederick Douglass National Historic Site. FRDO246. Photo by Carol M. Highsmith.

Frederick Douglass, his second wife Helen Pitts Douglass (right), and her
sister Eva Pitts (center). Courtesy National Park Service, Museum
Management Program and Frederick Douglass National Historic Site.
FRDO3912. Photo by Carol M. Highsmith.

a younger white woman, Helen Pitts, who had been his secretary at the Recorder of Deeds Office. Scholars have observed considerable strain in Douglass's first marriage on account of Anna Murray's discomfort in socializing with her husband's predominately white, well-educated, and female admirers. These domestic strains also seemed to have troubled Douglass's relationship with most of his adult children, who also struggled to match their father's success in a still heavily racist society. His children had difficulty accepting Helen into the family, but in time their relationship became cordial if not intimate. This family situation was not helped when some other black leaders publicly criticized Douglass for marrying outside his race.[69]

Ever the proper Victorian, Douglass rarely commented publicly on such private matters. His lectures and speeches, however, reveal a Douglass who thought deeply on questions of racial identity. He frequently commented on the mistreatment of recent immigrants, particularly the Chinese, and on the dire prospects of Native Americans on the dwindling frontier. Despite his personal experience of prejudice, Douglass remained confident that the nation ultimately would resolve its racial tensions, predicting that "Races and varieties of the human family appear and disappear, but humanity remains and will remain forever."[70]

In 1881, Douglass returned for the third time to writing an autobiography, *Life and Times of Frederick Douglass*. Rather than picking up where the 1855 concluded, Douglass prepared a new account of his life from his slave childhood to his current position as the nation's best-known and most influential African American. Douglass hoped that his life story would help reassure other African Americans that literacy, temperance, thrift, and hard work could surmount any obstacles posed by white racial prejudices. Modern scholars have recognized and frequently criticized the consciously Franklin-esque portrayal by Douglass of his rise from lowly origins. Likewise, *Life and Times* also has been dismissed for its sometimes clumsy prose style and its author's defensive account of his public career.[71] David Blight, however, applauds Douglass's last autobiography as well as his later speeches for resisting the popular tide toward sectional reconciliation in the 1880s and 1890s that required disavowing the painful history of slavery.[72]

Diplomat

Perhaps to escape the controversy surrounding their marriage, Douglass and Helen departed on a lengthy honeymoon tour of Europe and the Middle East in September 1886. During these travels, Douglass had enjoyable reunions with many aging colleagues from the abolitionist days, including Julia Griffiths, his former editorial assistant, who had returned to live in her native England. The Douglasses eventually moved on to visit many important historical landmarks in France, Italy, and Greece. The high point of this tour for Douglass was a stop in Egypt. Douglass got to view Africa firsthand and climbed to the top of the Pyramid of Cheops. This last stop enhanced Douglass's appreciation of the African contributions to classical civilization. Douglass also had the opportunity to leave numerous discerning observations about both the modern European and the classical worlds. Foreign travel also reinforced Douglass's core belief in unity of mankind. He told a Washington audience on his return to the United States, "In the East as in the West; in Egypt as in America; in all the world human nature is the same. Conditions may vary but the nature of man is permanent."[73]

Soon after his return to Washington, Douglass campaigned vigorously for the election of Benjamin Harrison, Indiana Republican, to the presidency. After Harrison won that office, he appointed Douglass to serve as the U.S. ambassador to the Caribbean island republic of Haiti. Some black leaders felt that Douglass had been slighted by the offer of this minor diplomatic post, but he regarded undertaking the appointment as a serious responsibility. According to McFeely, Douglass regarded Haiti as the symbol of "the liberation and autonomy of black people" and did not want it "exposed to the contempt of an insensitive white minister."[74]

The history of Haiti throughout the nineteenth century was one of political instability. It was Douglass's job to represent the United States before the government of Florvil Hyppolite, who had come to power after a bloody civil war. The United States had given crucial assistance to Hyppolite in that conflict and now expected him to comply with their request for the long-term lease of a naval coaling station at

Frederick Douglass with Madam Hyppolite in Haiti. Courtesy National Park Service, Museum Management Program and Frederick Douglass National Historic Site. FRDO157. Photo by Carol M. Highsmith.

Môle-Saint-Nicholas in the northwest corner of the country. Douglass loyally presented the American request for control of the Môle to the Haitian government. Fearing this to be only the first of many such requests for concessions, Hyppolite stalled in responding. Impatient, the Harrison administration dispatched the Atlantic fleet to Haitian waters, and its admiral assumed direction of the Môle negotiations from Douglass. When Hyppolite continued to resist, Harrison allowed the crisis to be defused by withdrawing the fleet. Douglass took this opportunity to resign his diplomatic post and later voiced his disapproval of all attempts to coerce the Haitians to cede territory against their will. Faced with inalterable Haitian opposition, the Harrison administration eventually gave up its pressure for a naval base lease.[75]

Lessons of the Hour

Douglass had been back at his Washington home from his diplomatic mission for only a year when he received a request from Hyppolite to serve the Haitian government. In 1892, a mammoth international fair, known as the World's Columbian Exposition was to be convened in Chicago to commemorate the four-hundredth anniversary of Christopher Columbus's first voyage to the New World. The Haitians funded a modest pavilion to display their agricultural and handicraft products. To head that pavilion and speak on behalf of Haiti at the numerous events planned during the year and-a-half-long exposition, President Hyppolite called on Douglass. This appointment demonstrates that the Haitians did not hold Douglass to blame for the bullying their country endured over the Môle-Saint-Nicholas at the hands of the Harrison administration.

Douglass accepted the post and along with Helen settled temporarily in Chicago. As anticipated, he made several major orations proclaiming the accomplishments of the Haitians and inferentially of all peoples of African descent. Douglass held up Haiti as an answer to charges of black inferiority, declaring, "The mission of Haiti was to dispel this degradation and dangerous delusion, and to give to the world a new and true revelation of the black man's character. This mission, she has performed and performed it well."[76]

During the exposition, Douglass also joined other blacks in protesting the lack of displays of any African American mechanical and intellectual achievements. Douglass furthermore used his time in Chicago to meet numerous younger blacks, such as Lawrence Dunbar, the poet, whom he encouraged to dedicate themselves to the cause of racial uplift.

One important acquaintance that Douglass made in Chicago was Ida B. Wells. A young journalist, Wells was struggling to expose the racist motivations of a recent wave of lynchings of Southern black males. Inspired by Wells's fervor, Douglass took up the antilynching cause. In his last years, he traveled widely to deliver his powerful "Lessons of the Hour" address, which vehemently denounced lynching. Even more significantly, Douglass rebuked prominent whites, such as Daniel H. Chamberlain, former South Carolina governor, and Frances Willard, temperance leader, for publicly condoning such outrages. He called on the North, and especially the Republican Party, to remember its commitment to the freedmen and to punish this antiblack barbarity. In his final advice to Americans, he declared, "Put away your racial prejudice. Banish the idea that one class must rule over another, recognize the fact that the rights of the humblest citizen are as worthy of protection as are those of the highest, and . . . your Republic will stand and flourish forever."[77] In what proved his last major address, Douglass demonstrated that he still possessed the same fire as he had in his youth to championing the right of his race to equal treatment in this nation without fear of censure or controversy.

IDA B. WELLS.

Ida B. Wells. From "Women of Distinction: Remarkable in Works and Invincible in Character" (published 1893). Manuscripts, Archives and Rare Books Division. Schomburg Center/Art Resource, N.Y.

The Legacy of Frederick Douglass

Politically active even in the face of his advancing years, Douglass attended a women's rights rally in Washington at the invitation of Susan B. Anthony on February 20, 1895. When he went home that evening, he prepared to attend another meeting at a neighborhood black church. Then, Douglass suddenly collapsed and quickly died of a heart attack. His passing was mourned nationwide. Five state legislatures adopted resolutions of official regret. Senators and a U.S. Supreme Court justice attended a memorial service for Douglass in Washington. He was buried in Rochester, and a heroic statue was erected near the site of his old house there.

As already noted, Douglass became a venerated symbol frequently called on during the civil rights struggles of the twentieth century. He also attracted critics. Just as the goals and tactics of the civil rights movement underwent vigorous debate during the 1960s, Douglass's legacy was sometimes attacked as too wedded to "interracialism, integrationism, and Americanism."[78] Although more than a century old, Douglass's own words make the strongest reply to modern-day detractors. His unwavering dedication to the rights guaranteed by the Constitution and to a broad definition of inherent human rights makes Douglass's message relevant to the struggles for liberty and equality still being waged today.

THE DOUGLASS FUNERAL.—Inside the Church.

The Douglass funeral: Inside. From the collection of the Rochester Public Library Local History Division.

Notes

1. Quoted in Herbert Aptheker, "DuBois on Douglass, 1895," *Journal of Negro History* 49(October 1964): 265, 267.

2. Booker T. Washington, *Frederick Douglass* (Philadelphia: George W. Jacobs, 1906), 338.

3. Moses J. Wilson, "Where Honor Is Due: Frederick Douglass as Representative Black Man," *Prospects* 17(1992): 177–88; Waldo E. Martin Jr., "Images of Frederick Douglass in the Afro-American Mind: The Recent Black Freedom Struggle," in *Frederick Douglass: New Literary and Historical Essays,* ed. Eric J. Sundquist, 277–79 (New York: Cambridge University Press, 1990); Peter C. Myers, *Frederick Douglass: Race and the Rebirth of American Liberalism* (Lawrence: University of Kansas Press, 2008), 1–7, 195–203.

4. As quoted in Martin, "Images of Frederick Douglass," 280.

5. Roy P. Basler, *The Lincoln Legend: A Study of Changing Conceptions* [1935] (New York: Octagon, 1969); Merrill Peterson, *The Jeffersonian Image in the American Mind* (New York: Oxford University Press, 1960); Marcus Cunliffe, *George Washington: Man and Monument* (Boston: Little, Brown, 1958); Thomas L. Connelly, *The Marble Man: Robert E. Lee and His Image in American Society* (New York: Knopf, 1977); Merrill D. Peterson, *John Brown: The Legend Revisited* (Charlottesville: University of Virginia Press, 2002); Stacey Schiff, "Desperate Seeking Susan," *New York Times,* October 16, 2006.

6. Nathan Irvin Huggins, *Slave and Citizen: The Life of Frederick Douglass* (Boston: Little, Brown, 1980), 4.

7. Dickson J. Preston, *Young Frederick Douglass: The Maryland Years* (Baltimore: Johns Hopkins University Press, 1980), 87.

8. John W. Blassingame and John R. McKivigan, eds., *The Frederick Douglass Papers,* ser. 2 (New Haven: Yale University Press, 1999–2011) [hereafter, *Douglass Papers,* ser. 2], 2:84.

9. William S. McFeely, *Frederick Douglass* (New York: W. W. Norton, 1991), 34.

10. *My Bondage and My Freedom,* in *Douglass Papers,* ser. 2, 2:141.

11. Waldo E. Martin Jr., *The Mind of Frederick Douglass* (Chapel Hill: University of North Carolina Press, 1984), 13.

12. Peter C. Myers, *Frederick Douglass: Race and the Rebirth of American Liberalism* (Lawrence: University of Kansas Press, 2008), 20–82.

13. *My Bondage and My Freedom,* in *Douglass Papers,* ser. 2, 2:188.

14. Alan J. Rice and Martin Crawford, *Liberating Sojourn: Frederick Douglass & Transatlantic Reform* (Athens: University of Georgia Press, 1999), 1.

15. McFeely, *Frederick Douglass,* 78.

16. *My Bondage and My Freedom,* in *Douglass Papers,* ser. 2, 2:200–201.

17. Merton L. Dillon, *Slavery Attacked: Southern Slaves and Their Allies, 1619–1865* (Baton Rouge: Louisiana State University Press, 1990), 5–27, 130–61; Peter P. Hinks, *To Awaken My Afflicted Brethren: David Walker and the Problem of Antebellum Slave Resistance* (University Park: Pennsylvania State University Press, 1997), 91–115.

18. James Brewer Stewart, *Holy Warriors: The Abolitionists and American Slavery* (New York: Hill and Wang, 1976), 35–96.

19. *My Bondage and My Freedom*, in *Douglass Papers*, ser. 2, 2:204.

20. Martin, *Mind of Frederick Douglass*, 22.

21. Gregory Lampe, *Frederick Douglass, Freedom's Voice* (East Lansing: Michigan State University Press, 1998), 57–96.

22. Isaac Nelson quoted in the 1846 Dublin edition of the *Narrative*. See *Douglass Papers*, ser. 2, 1:xxxix.

23. Harold Bloom, ed., *Modern Critical Interpretations: Frederick Douglass's Narrative of the Life of Frederick Douglass* (New York: Chelsea House, 1988); William L. Andrews, *To Tell a Free Story: The First Century of Afro-American Autobiography* (Urbana: University of Illinois Press, 1986), 214–39; Deborah McDowell, "In the First Place: Frederick Douglass and the Afro-American Tradition," in *Critical Essays on Frederick Douglass*, ed. William L. Andrews (Boston: G. K. Hall, 1991), 192–214; Henry Louis Gates, "From Wheatley to Douglass: The Politics of Displacement," in *Frederick Douglass: New Literary and Historical Essays*, ed. Eric J. Sundquist (New York: Cambridge University Press, 1990), 47–65.

24. Speech: "Principles of Temperance Reform," March 5, 1848, in *The Frederick Douglass Papers*, ser. 1, ed. John W. Blassingame and John R. McKivigan (New Haven: Yale University Press, 1979–1992) [hereafter, *Douglass Papers*, ser. 1], 2:107.

25. Speech: "Slavery Corrupts American Society and Religion," October 17, 1845, *Douglass Papers*, ser. 1, 1:51.

26. David W. Blight, *Frederick Douglass' Civil War: Keeping the Faith in Jubilee* (Baton Rouge: Louisiana State University Press, 1991), 118–21.

27. John R. McKivigan and Jason H. Silverman, "Monarchial Liberty and Republican Slavery: West Indies Emancipation Celebrations in Upstate New York and Canada West," *Afro-Americans in New York Life and History* 19 (January 1986): 7–18.

28. Rice and Crawford, *Liberating Sojourn*, 3.

29. Martin, *Mind of Frederick Douglass*, 31–32.

30. *Life and Times*, in *Douglass Papers*, ser. 2, 3:206–207.

31. Quoted in Stewart, *Holy Warriors*, 149.

32. This relationship is skillfully examined in John Stauffer, *The Black Hearts of Men: Radical Abolitionists and the Transformation of Race* (Cambridge, Mass.: Harvard University Press, 2002), 61–64, 278–79. Also see John R.

McKivigan, "The Frederick Douglass-Gerrit Smith Friendship and Political Abolitionism in the 1850s," in *Frederick Douglass: New Literary and Historical Essays*, ed. Eric J. Sundquist (New York: Cambridge University Press, 1990), 205–32.

33. Speech: "The Anti-Slavery Movement," March 19, 1855, *Douglass Papers*, ser. I, 3:19–20.

34. Ibid., 3:45.

35. Robert B. Stepto, "Storytelling in Early Afro-American Fiction: 'Frederick Douglass' 'The Heroic Slave.'" *Georgia Review* 36 (summer 1982): 355–68.

36. McFeely, *Frederick Douglass*, 181.

37. Eric J. Sundquist, ed., *Frederick Douglass: New Literary and Historical Essays* (New York: Cambridge University Press, 1990), 11.

38. Phyllis F. Field, *The Politics of Race in New York: The Struggle for Black Suffrage in the Civil War Era* (Ithaca: Cornell University Press, 1982), 35–37.

39. Robert S. Levine, *Martin Delany, Frederick Douglass, and the Politics of Representative Identity* (Chapel Hill: University of North Carolina Press, 1997), 58–98.

40. Robert Stepto, "Sharing the Thunder: The Literary Exchanges of Harriet Beecher Stowe, Henry Bibb, and Frederick Douglass," in *New Essays on Uncle Tom's Cabin*, ed. Eric J. Sundquist (New York: Cambridge University Press, 1986), 136–37, 143–52; Levine, *Martin Delany, Frederick Douglass*, 83–85.

41. Levine, *Martin Delany, Frederick Douglass*, 82–83.

42. *My Bondage and My Freedom*, in *Douglass Papers*, ser. 2, 2:185. See also Rosetta Douglass, *My Mother as I Recall Her: A Paper Read before Anna Murray Douglass Union, W.C.T.U., May 10, 1900* (Washington, D.C.: National Association of Colored Women, 1923), 14; McFeely, *Frederick Douglass*, 172.

43. Speech: "What to the Slave Is the Fourth of July?" July 5, 1852, *Douglass Papers*, ser. I, 2:376.

44. David S. Reynolds, *John Brown, Abolitionist: The Man Who Killed Slavery, Sparked the Civil War, and Seeded Civil Rights* (New York: Vintage Books, 2005), 95–137; Stephen B. Oates *To Purge This Land with Blood: A Biography of John Brown* (Amherst: University of Massachusetts Press, 1970), 97–18; McFeely, *Frederick Douglass*, 192.

45. Blight, *Frederick Douglass' Civil War*, 95–96. See also Leslie Friedman Goldstein, "Violence as an Instrument for Social Change: The Views of Frederick Douglass (1817–1895)," *Journal of Negro History* 61 (January 1976): 61–66.

46. Editorial: "John Brown Not Insane," *Douglass' Monthly*, November 1859; Myers, *Frederick Douglass*, 225–26n.

47. Speech: "John Brown and the Slaveholders' Insurrection," January 30, 1860, *Douglass Papers*, ser. I, 3:317.

48. Speech: "Did John Brown Fail?" May 30, 1881, *Douglass Papers*, ser. I, 5:21.

49. Leslie Friedman Goldstein, "Morality & Prudence in the Statesmanship of Frederick Douglass: Radical as Reformer," *Polity* 16, no. 4 (summer 1984), 620; Martin, *Mind of Frederick Douglass*, 35; Myers, *Frederick Douglass*, 96, 101; Blight, *Frederick Douglass' Civil War*, 57–58; McFeely, *Frederick Douglass*, 208; Stauffer, *Black Hearts of Men*, 278.

50. Speech: "The Mission of the War," January 13, 1864, *Douglass Papers*, ser. I, 4:6.

51. Blight, *Frederick Douglass' Civil War*, 235.

52. Speech: "Negroes and the National War Effort," July 6, 1863, in *The Frederick Douglass Papers*, ser. 3, ed. John R. McKivigan (New Haven: Yale University Press, 2009) [hereafter *Douglass Papers*, ser. 3], 3:596.

53. *Life and Times*, in *Douglass Papers*, ser. 2, 3:281.

54. Stauffer, *Black Hearts of Men*, 279.

55. Eric Foner, *Reconstruction: America's Unfinished Revolution, 1863–1877* (New York: Harper & Row, 1988), 176–227.

56. Myers, *Frederick Douglass*, 130–32.

57. Speech: "Sources of Danger to the Republic," February 7, 1867, *Douglass Papers*, ser. I, 4:164.

58. Carl R. Osthaus, *Freedmen, Philanthropy, and Fraud: A History of the Freedman's Savings Bank* (Urbana: University of Illinois Press, 1976), 183.

59. Washington, *Frederick Douglass*, 292.

60. Speech: "The Republican Party Must Be Maintained in Power," April 13, 1872, *Douglass Papers*, ser. I, 4:298. See also Foner, *Reconstruction*, 412–59.

61. Speech: "There Was a Right Side in the Late War," May 30, 1878, *Douglass Papers*, ser. I, 4:491. See also Donald Barr Chidsey, *The Gentleman from New York: A Life of Roscoe Conkling* (New Haven: Yale University Press, 1935), 209–93.

62. Speech: "I Am a Radical Woman Suffrage Man," May 28, 1888, *Douglass Papers*, ser. I, 5:387.

63. Speech: "Give Women Fair Play," March 31, 1888, *Douglass Papers*, ser. I, 5:355.

64. As quoted in John R. McKivigan, *Forgotten Firebrand: James Redpath and the Making of Nineteenth-Century America* (Ithaca: Cornell University Press, 2008), 122.

65. Speech: "The Blessings of Liberty and Education," September 3, 1894, *Douglass Papers*, ser. I, 5:623.

66. Martin, *Mind of Frederick Douglass*, 26–27.

67. Speech: "The Negro Exodus from the Gulf States," September 12, 1879, *Douglass Papers*, ser. I, 4:527.

68. As quoted in Myers, *Frederick Douglass*, 159. For an unsympathetic appraisal of Douglass's view of the Exoduster movement, see Nell I. Painter, *Exodusters: Black Migration to Kansas after Reconstruction* (New York: W. W. Norton, 1976), 249.

69. McFeely, *Frederick Douglass*, 310–11, 320.

70. Speech: "Our Composite Nationality," December 7, 1869, *Douglass Papers*, ser. I, 4:245. See also Martin, *Mind of Frederick Douglass*, 197–251.

71. McFeely, *Frederick Douglass*, 311–12; Sundquist, *Frederick Douglass*, 4.

72. David W. Blight, *Race and Reunion: The Civil War in American* Memory (Cambridge, Mass.: Belknap Press of Harvard University, 2001), 311–19. See also William L. Andrews, "Reunion in the Postbellum Slave Narrative: Frederick Douglass and Elizabeth Keckley," *Black American Literature Forum*, 23(spring 1989): 7.

73. Speech: "My Foreign Travels," December 15, 1887, *Douglass Papers*, ser. I, 5:328.

74. McFeely, *Frederick Douglass*, 336.

75. *Life and Times*, in *Douglass Papers*, ser. 2, 3:439–57; McFeely, *Frederick Douglass*, 334–58.

76. Speech: "Haiti and the Haitian People," January 2, 1893, Douglass Papers, ser. I, 5:529.

77. Speech: "Lessons of the Hour," January 9, 1894, *Douglass Papers*, ser. I, 5:607.

78. Martin, "Images of Frederick Douglass," 280–82. See also Vincent Harding, *There Is a River: The Black Struggle for Freedom in America* (New York: Harcourt Brace, 1981), 167; Wilson, "Where Honor Is Due," 177–88.

FREDERICK DOUGLASS
CHRONOLOGY

1818
Born Frederick Augustus Washington Bailey in February at Holme Hill Farm, Talbot County, Md.

1826
Douglass sent to live with Hugh Auld's family in Baltimore.

1833
Master loans Douglass to Thomas Auld at St. Michaels, Md.

1834
Douglass spends a year as a fieldhand hired out to Edward Covey, Talbot County "slave breaker."

1836
After Douglass's unsuccessfully attempts to escape, he is returned to Hugh Auld in Baltimore.

1838

On September 3, Douglass departs Baltimore on a successful escape attempt to the North. He marries Anna Murray in New York City on September 15, and the couple settles in New Bedford, Mass.

1841

After addressing an antislavery meeting in Nantucket, Mass., Douglass is hired as a lecturer by Garrisonian abolitionists.

1845

Douglass publishes his first autobiography, *Narrative of the Life of Frederick Douglass, an American Slave,* placing himself in danger of being hunted and recaptured as a runaway slave. For his safety, Douglass departs in August for twenty-one months in Great Britain as an abolitionist lecturer.

1847

From his new home in Rochester, N.Y., Douglass publishes the first issue of his weekly newspaper *North Star* on December 3.

1848

Douglass attends the Seneca Falls Women's Rights Convention on July 19–20.

1851

After breaking from the Garrisonian abolitionists, Douglass revamps his newspaper into the *Frederick Douglass' Paper,* a Liberty Party vehicle.

1852

Douglass publishes his novella, "The Heroic Slave." On July 5, he delivers his most memorable oration, "What to the Slave Is the Fourth of July?" in Rochester, N.Y.

1855

Douglass's second autobiography, *My Bondage and My Freedom*, is published.

1859

Following Harpers Ferry Raid in October, Douglass flees first to Canada and then Great Britain for safety because of his prior close connections with John Brown, the head plotter. Douglass is not able to return home until April 1860.

1863

After recruiting black troops for the Union Army, Douglass has the first of three private interviews with President Abraham Lincoln. Douglass encourages Lincoln to allow black soldiers to demonstrate their abilities in combat against the Confederates.

1870

Douglass relocates to Washington, D.C., and begins editing the *New National Era* to advance black civil rights as well as other reforms.

1871

Douglass serves as assistant secretary on the U.S. Commission sent to Santo Domingo to evaluate prospects for annexation.

1874

Appointed president of the Freedman's Savings Bank in March, Douglass has to close the institution as insolvent in July.

1877

President Ruther B. Hayes appoints Douglass U.S. marshal of the District of Columbia.

1881

President James A. Garfield appoints Douglass recorder of the deeds for the District of Columbia. Douglass publishes his third autobiography, *The Life and Times of Frederick Douglass.*

1882

In August, Douglass's wife Anna dies.

1884

Douglass's marriage in January to a younger white woman, Helen Pitts, causes a public controversy.

1886

In September, Douglass and his new wife depart for tour of Europe and the Near East, returning in August 1887.

1889

Douglass accepts an appointment as U.S. ambassador to Haiti in July. He resigns post in August 1889 after clashes with the Benjamin Harrison administration over attempted annexation of a Haitian port to serve as an American naval base.

1892

While serving as commissioner of the Haitian pavilion at the World's Columbian Exposition in Chicago from October to December 1893, Douglass meets many of the next generation of African American leaders.

1895

Douglass dies at his Cedar Hill home in Washington, D.C., on February 20 after attending a women's rights convention.

THE WORDS OF FREDERICK DOUGLASS

Abolition
(see also Colonization, Emancipation)

The real and only-to-be-relied-on movement for the abolition of slavery in this country, and throughout the world, is a great moral and religious movement. The work of which is, the enlightenment of the public mind, the quickening and enlightening of the dead conscience of the nation into life, and to a sense of the gross injustice, fraud, wrong and inhumanity of enslaving their fellow-men,—the fixing in the soul of the nation an invincible abhorrence of the whole system of slaveholding; and begetting in it a firm and inflexible determination to rid itself of its guiltiness in the matter. My means for the attainment of this deeply-desired and long-prayed-for end, are the simple proclamation of the word of Truth, written and spoken in the love of it, and in faith believing that the God of truth will give it success.

—Correspondence: Douglass to William Lloyd Garrison, October 27, 1844, *Douglass Papers,* ser. 3, 1:33

Yet the cause shall not suffer; the star, whose feeble light had become painful, shall yet become a sun, whose brilliant rays shall scorch, blister and burn, till slavery shall be utterly consumed.

—Correspondence: Douglass to William Lloyd Garrison, September 16, 1845, *Douglass Papers*, ser. 3, 1:53

It is clear that Slavery in our country can only be abolished by creating a public opinion favorable to its abolition, and this can only be done by enlightening the Public mind—by exposing the character of slavery and enforcing the great principle of justice and humanity against it. To do this with what ability I may possess is plainly my duty. To shrink from doing so, on any fitting occasion, from a mere fear of giving offence to those implicated in the wickedness, would be to betray the sacred trust committed to me, and to act the part of a coward.

—Correspondence: Douglass to Thurlow Weed, December 1, 1845, *Douglass Papers*, ser. 3, 1:67–68

Let slavery be hemmed in on every side by the moral and religious sentiments of mankind, and its death is certain.

—Correspondence: Douglass to William Lloyd Garrison, April 16, 1846, *Douglass Papers*, ser. 3, 1:110

I expose slavery . . . because to expose it is to kill it. Slavery is one of those monsters of darkness to whom the light of truth is death.

—Speech: "American Slavery, American Religion, and the Free Church of Scotland," May 22, 1846, *Douglass Papers*, ser. 1, 1:294

Fellow-citizens! I will not enlarge further on your national inconsistencies. The existence of slavery in this country brands your republicanism as a sham, your humanity as a base pretense, and your

Christianity as a lie. It destroys your moral power abroad; it corrupts your politicians at home.

—Speech: "What to the Slave Is the Fourth of July?" July 5, 1852, *Douglass Papers*, ser. I, 2:383

The Anti-Slavery movement has little to entitle it to being called a new thing under the sun in view of any just historical test. I know nothing original about it. Its ideas and arguments were already to the hand of the present work-men; the oldest abolitionist of to-day is but the preacher of a faith, frames and practised long before he was born. The patriots of the American Revolution clearly saw, and with all their inconsistency, they had the grace to confess, the abhorrent character of Slavery, and to hopefully predict its overthrow and complete extirpation. Washington, and Jefferson, Patrick Henry, and Luther Martin, Franklin, and Adams, Madison, and Monroe, and a host of earnest Statesmen, Jurists, Scholars, and Divines of the country, were among those who looked forward to this happy consummation.

—Speech: "The Anti-Slavery Movement," March 18, 1855, *Douglass Papers*, ser. I, 3:21

The difference between abolitionists and those by whom they are opposed, is not as to principles. All are agreed in respect to these. The manner of applying them is the point of difference.

—Speech: "The Anti-Slavery Movement," March 18, 1855, *Douglass Papers*, ser. I, 3:46

Generations unborn will envy us the felicity of having been born at a time when such noble work could be accomplished, when the foundations can be laid deep and strong for the future liberation of the race.

—Editorial: "The Do-Nothing Policy," *Frederick Douglass' Paper*, September 12, 1856

Blacks

Remember that we are one, that our cause is one, that we must help each other, if we would succeed. We have drank to the dregs the bitter cup of slavery; we have worn the heavy yoke; we have sighed beneath our bonds, and writhed beneath the bloody lash;—cruel mementoes of our oneness are indelibly marked in our living flesh. We are one with you under the ban of prejudice and proscription—one with you under the slander of inferiority—one with you in social and political disfranchisement. What you suffer, we suffer; what you endure, we endure. We are indissolubly united, and must fall or flourish together.

—Editorial "To Our Oppressed Countrymen," *North Star,* December 3, 1847

Disunionism

I welcome the bolt, either from the North or the South, which shall shatter this Union; for under this Union lie the prostrate forms of three millions with whom I am identified. In consideration of their wrongs, of their sufferings, of their groans, I welcome the bolt, either from the celestial or the infernal regions, which shall sever this Union in twain.

—Speech: "Love of God, Love of Man, Love of Country," September 24, 1847, *Douglass Papers,* ser. I, 2:95

Persecution

"To make war upon the church of the living God." What less than the flames off hell is an adequate punishment for such a heaven-daring crime? What! speak evil of the men who minister at the altar as the Most High? For such reckless wickedness—for such sacrilegious temerity, let his character be blasted forever, brand him infidel, stamp him an atheist, call his disorganizer, and warn the world against him as a moist dangerous man. Such is bit a faint picture of the malignity of religious persecution, as it is at this moment carried on against the abolitionists.

—Editorial: "American Religion and American Slavery," *North Star*, June 17, 1850

Violent Tactics

The only way to make the Fugitive Slave Law a dead letter, is to make a few dead slave-catchers. There is no need to kill them either—shoot them in the legs, and send them to the South [as] living epistles of the free gospel preached here at the North.

—Speech: "John Brown's Contributions to the Abolition Movement," December 3, 1860, *Douglass Papers*, ser. I, 3:419

Women

They filled me with admiration, as I viewed them occupying their noble position; a few women, almost alone in a community of thousands, asserting truths and living out principles at once hated and feared by almost the entire community; and doing all this with a composure and serenity of soul which would well compare with the most experienced champion and standard bearer of our cause, Friend Garrison himself. Heaven bless them, and continue them strength to withstand all trials through which their principles may call them to pass.

—Correspondence: Douglass to James Miller McKim, September 5, 1844, *Douglass Papers*, ser. 3, 1:28

When the true history of the antislavery cause shall be written, woman will occupy a large space in its pages, for the cause of the slave has been peculiarly woman's cause.

—Autobiography: *Life and Times*, 1881, p. 367

Observing woman's agency, devotion and efficiency in pleading the cause of the slave, gratitude for this high service early moved me to give favorable attention to the subject of what is called "Woman's Rights" and caused me to be denominated a woman's-rights-man. I am glad to say I have never been ashamed to be thus designated.

—Autobiography: *Life and Times*, 1881, p. 370

African American Character

One thing is certain—whether we are capable, or have natural abilities to rise from a condition in life to a higher state of civilization—these questions cannot be answered for us: they must be answered by ourselves. We must show them what we are capable of becoming—show them we are skilled architects, profound thinkers, originators or discovers of ideas, and other things connected with a higher state of civilization. This will be of far more importance than all the lectures ever delivered in our favor by our white friends. This would be a fact plain enough to be understood by the simplest mind. This is what is wanted to abolish chattel slavery. When we can point to intellects among the blacks as bright as that of Webster, Clay, or Calhoun—when we can do this, but not till then—is our case made out.

—Speech: "These Questions Cannot Be Answered by the White Race," May 11, 1855, *Douglass Papers*, ser. I, 3:88

The idea prevails everywhere in this country that, as a people, however much we may talk of our love of liberty, and the regard of our rights and a knowledge of our rights there is a deep-seated conviction in the public mind that we care too little about them when assailed by force. I would have every colored man defend them when the law does not protect him, and surrender his liberty only with his life. I would have you fight for your liberty when assailed by the slave hunter. This will gain you some respect. Hungarians, Irishmen and Italians can fight for liberty, and they are respected, and once in a while a colored man does the same, and is respected for it. Fear inculcates respect. I would rather see insurrection for the next six months in the South than that slavery should exist there for [the] next six years. Anthony Burns would never have gone back to slavery of he had had the spirit to fight for his liberty.

—Speech: "These Questions Cannot Be Answered by the White Race," May 11, 1855, *Douglass Papers*, ser. I, 3:88

I hold that next to the dignity of being a freeman, is the dignity of striving to be free. I detest the slaveholder, and almost equally detest a contented slave. They are both enemies to freedom. We shall have gained immensely for our cause as a people, when we have shown a proper sense of the wrongs which we suffer as a people.

—Speech: "Citizenship and the Spirit of Caste," May 11, 1858, *Douglass Papers*, ser. I, 3:210

No people are more talked about and no people seem more imperfectly understood. Those who see us every day seem not to know us.

—Editorial: "The Races," *Douglass' Monthly*, August 1859

Colored people have had something to do with almost everything of vital importance in the life and progress of this great country. We have never forsaken the white man in any great emergency, and never expect to forsake him.

—Editorial: "Why Should a Colored Man Enlist?" *Douglass' Monthly*, April 1863

We have undertaken . . . a new experiment [concerning] the possibility or impossibility of all nations, kindreds, tongues, and peoples living harmoniously . . . under one government.
—Editorial: "We Need a True, Strong, and Principled Party," *New National Era*, March 29, 1871

Slavery was a poor school in which to prepare statesmen, but a race which has gone through what we have cannot be blotted out nor kept down.
—Speech: "The South Knows Us." May 4, 1879, *Douglass Papers*, ser. I, 4:499–500

We will never change our relations to the white people until we become more economical, stick to our employment and live within our means. If you do people will respect you.
—Speech: "The South Knows Us." May 4, 1879, *Douglass Papers*, ser. I, 4:502

The negro, as already intimated, is preeminently a Southern man. He is so both in constitution and habits, in body as well as in mind.
—Speech: "The Negro Exodus from the Gulf States," September 12, 1879, *Douglass Papers*, ser. I, 4:530

We negroes are an irrepressible people, and there is no keeping us back.
—Speech: "Black Teachers for Black Pupils," December 4, 1879, *Douglass Papers*, ser. I, 4:544

Alcohol

[At the New Year] Sober people look both ways at the beginning of the year, surveying the errors of the past, and providing against possible errors of the future.
—Autobiography: *My Bondage and My Freedom*, 1855, p. 154

Drinking by Slaves

A slave who would work during the holidays was considered by our masters as scarcely deserving them. He was regarded as one who rejected the favor of his master. It was deemed a disgrace not to get drunk at Christmas; and he was regarded as lazy indeed, who had not provided himself with the necessary means, during the year, to get him whiskey enough to last him through Christmas.

—Autobiography: *Narrative*, 1845, p. 55

I have had some experience of intemperance as well as of slavery. In the Southern States, masters induce their slaves to drink whisky, in order to keep them from devising ways and means by which to obtain their freedom. In order to make a man a slave, it is necessary to silence or drown his mind. It is not the flesh that objects to being bound—it is the spirit. It is not the mere animal part—it is the immortal mind which distinguishes man from brute creation. To blind his affections, it is necessary to bedim and bedizzy his understanding. In no other way can this be so well accomplished as by using ardent spirits! On Saturday evening, it is the custom of the slaveholder to give his slave drink, and why? because if they had time to think, if left to reflection on the Sabbath day, they might devise means by which to obtain their liberty.

—Speech: "Temperance and Anti-Slavery," March 30, 1846, *Douglass Papers*, ser. I, I:207

Temperance

I was not a slave to intemperance, but a slave to my fellow-men.

—Speech: "Intemperance and Slavery," October 20, 1845, *Douglass Papers*, ser. I, I:56

Teetotalism has been an interesting subject to me. We have a large class of free people of color in America; that class has, through the influence of intemperance, done much to retard the progress of the anti-slavery movement—that is, they have furnished arguments to the oppressors for oppressing us; they have pointed to the drunkards among the free colored population, and asked us the question, tauntingly—"What better would you be if you were in their situation?" This of course was a great grievance to me. I set my voice against intemperance. I lectured against it, and talked against it, in the street, in the wayside, at the fire-place; wherever I went during the last seven years, my voice his been against intemperance.

—Speech: "Intemperance and Slavery," October 20, 1845, *Douglass Papers*, ser. I, 1:56

I am pledged against the use of ardent spirits, because they have the same effect upon a black man that they produce upon a white man. And . . . if I had no other evidence of my perfect identity with the human family, than the fact, that these liquors make a black man drunk in common with a white man, it would be sufficient to perpetuate all the pretensions I have ever had to my equal humanity.

—Speech: "The Temperance in America and Britain," May 21, 1846, *Douglass Papers*, ser. I, 1:265–66

But more strictly as regards temperance, I consider sometimes that I have a right to speak on this question, for I was once fond of a little drop occasionally, and when I have been indulging in this way, I have also felt myself to be some very great man—something like a governor or president. However, I did not continue long in these practices; and I have been able, by the blessing of God, for the last seven years, to steer entirely clear of them.

—Speech: "The Temperance in America and Britain," May 21, 1846, *Douglass Papers*, ser. I, 1:267

Animals

There is no successful farming without well-trained and well-treated horses and oxen, and one of the greatest pleasures connected with agricultural life may be found in the pleasant relations capable of subsisting between the farmer and his four-legged companions; for they are company as well as helpers in his toil.

—Speech: "Agriculture and Black Progress," September 18, 1873, *Douglass Papers*, ser. I, 4:388

Aristocracy
(see also *Class*)

We have here an aristocracy of skin [which bestows] the high privilege of insulting a colored man with the most perfect impunity.

—Correspondence: Douglass to John T. Delane, Editor of the London *Times*, June 29, 1850, *Douglass Papers*, ser. 3, 1:421

We affect contempt for the castes and aristocracies of the old world and laugh at their assumptions, but at home foster pretensions far less rational and much more ridiculous.

—Autobiography: *Life and Times*, 1881, p. 393

Art

Man is the only picture-making animal in the world. He alone of all inhabitants of the earth has the capacity and passion for pictures.

—Speech: "Pictures and Progress," December 3, 1861, *Douglass Papers*, ser. I, 3:459

There are some things and places made sacred by their uses and by the events with which they are associated, especially those which have in any measure changed the current of human taste, thought and life, or which have revealed new powers and triumphs of the human soul.

    —Autobiography: *Life and Times,* 1881, 419

Assimilation

(see also Diversity, Immigration)

There is but one destiny, it seems to me, left for us, and that is to make ourselves and be made by others a part of the American people in every sense of the word. Assimilation and not isolation is our true policy and our natural destiny. Unification for us is life; separation is death. We cannot afford to set up for ourselves a separate political party, or adopt for ourselves a political creed apart from the rest of our fellow citizens. Our own interests will be subserved by a generous care for the interests of the Nation at large. All the political, social and literary forces around us tend to unification.

    —Speech: "Our Destiny Is Largely in Our Own Hands," April 16, 1883, *Douglass Papers,* ser. I, 5:80

Autobiography

It is far easier to write about others than about one's self. . . . Time and events have summoned me to stand forth both as a witness and an advocate for a people long dumb, not allowed to speak for themselves, yet much misunderstood, and deeply wronged.

    —Autobiography: *Life and Times,* 1881, p. 375

No man liveth unto himself, or ought to live unto himself. My life has conformed to this Bible saying, for, more than most men, I have been the thin edge of the wedge to open, for my people a way in many directions and places never before occupied by them.

—Autobiography: *Life and Times*, 1881, p. 377

To revisit places, scenes and friends after forty years is not a very common occurrence in the lives of men, and while the desire to do so may be intense, the gratification has to it a sad side as well as a cheerful one. The old people first met there have passed away, the middle aged have grown old, and the young have only heard their fathers and mothers speak of you. The places are there, but the people are gone.

—Autobiography: *Life and Times*, 1881, p. 409

Boasting

Contemplating my life as a whole, I have to say that, although it has at times been dark and stormy, and I have met with hardships from which other men have been exempted, yet my life has in many respects been remarkably full of sunshine and joy. Servitude, persecution, false friends, desertion and depreciation, have not robbed my life of happiness or made it a burden. I have been, and still am, especially fortunate and may well indulge sentiments of warmest gratitude for the lines in which my life has fallen. While I cannot boast of having accomplished great things in the world, I cannot on the other hand feel that I have lived in vain.

—Autobiography: *Life and Times*, 1881, p. 457

Capital Punishment
(see also Human Rights)

Murder is not the cure for murder—lying and stealing will not cure lying and stealing. The old doctrine was; "An eye for an eye—a tooth for a tooth"—but that was the doctrine of a by-gone age and generation, and not of this one of light, intelligence and reason.

—Speech: "Capital Punishment Is a Mockery of Justice," October 7, 1858, *Douglass Papers,* ser. I, 3:244

But in the name of all things sacred—to Heaven and earth—must we hang a man for no better reason than that if we let him live he may be pardoned and restored to society? Is there no other way of preventing the pardoning power? Are we reduced to the necessity of killing a man to place him beyond the reach of mercy? What a confession in this of the impotency of the people, if the pardoning power is upon the whole dangerous and mischievous, the power is with the people. Let them change it; but for mercy's sake, let not the fear that mercy may be shown be an apology for hanging.

—Speech: "Capital Punishment Is a Mockery of Justice," October 7, 1858, *Douglass Papers,* ser. I, 3:245

Children

Of all consciences, let me have those to deal with which have not been bewildered by the cares of life. I do not remember ever to have met with a *boy,* while I was in slavery, who defended the slave system; but I have often had boys to console me, with the hope that something would yet occur, by which I might be made free.

—Autobiography: *My Bondage and My Freedom,* 1855, p. 59

Christmas

From what I know of the effect of these holidays upon the slave, I believe them to be among the most effective means in the hands of the slaveholder in keeping down the spirit of insurrection. . . . These holidays serve as conductors, or safety-valves, to carry off the rebellious spirit of enslaved humanity.

  —Autobiography: *Narrative,* 1845,p. 55

The holidays are part and parcel of the gross fraud, wrong, and inhumanity of slavery. . . . Their object seems to be, to disgust their slaves with freedom, by plunging them into the lowest depths of dissipation. . . . when the holidays ended, we staggered up from the filth of our wallowing, took a long breath, and marched to the field,—feeling, upon the whole, rather glad to go, from what our master had deceived us into a belief was freedom, back to the arms of slavery.

  —Autobiography: *Narrative,* 1845, p. 56

To enslave men, successfully and safely, it is necessary to have their minds occupied with thoughts and aspirations short of the liberty of which they are deprived. A certain degree of attainable good must be kept before them. These holidays serve the purpose of keeping the minds of the slaves occupied with prospective pleasure, within the limits of slavery.

  —Autobiography: *My Bondage and My Freedom,* 1855, p. 144

Cities

Great cities, like great men, have their distinctive, individual characters and qualities. While all have something in common, each has something peculiar to itself, and each makes its own peculiar impression on the outside world. New York is not Boston, nor is Boston Philadelphia; and neither one nor the other is Washington.

—Speech: "Our National Capital," May 8, 1877, *Douglass Papers*, ser. I, 4:450

Paris

The very name of Paris starts a thousand reflections. She is a city of fame, fashion and fancy; a city of taste and terrors; of heroes and horrors; of beauty, barricades, and battles; of varied and startling vicissitudes—some of them so violent and destructive that we wonder that she has not perished long ago by her own internal fires; yet here she stands in all her strength and beauty.

—Speech: "My Foreign Travels," December 15, 1887, *Douglass Papers*, ser. I, 5:294

Philadelphia

We were marching through a city remarkable for the depth and bitterness of its hatred of the abolition movement; a city whose populace had mobbed anti-slavery meetings, burned temperance halls and churches owned by colored people, and burned down Pennsylvania Hall because it had opened its doors to people of different colors upon terms of equality. But now the children of those who had committed these outrages and follies, were applauding the very principles which their fathers had condemned.

—Autobiography: *Life and Times*, 1881, p. 306

Rome

The men who made Rome worth going to see were the men who stayed there.

—Speech: "The South Knows Us," May 4, 1879, *Douglass Papers*, ser. I, 4:501

Empires, principalities, powers and dominions have perished; alters and their gods have mingled with the dust; a religion which made men virtuous in peace and invincible in war, has perished or been supplanted, yet the Eternal City itself remains.
    —Autobiography: *Life and Times,* 1881, p. 421

[T]he causes of the decline and fall of the Roman Empire. The lap of luxury and the pursuit of ease and pleasure are death to manly courage, energy, will and enterprise.
    —Autobiography: *Life and Times,* 1881, p. 422

Religion seems to be in Rome the chief business by which men live.
    —Autobiography: *Life and Times,* 1881, p. 423

Here, according to the age and body of its times, human ambition reached its topmost height and human power its utmost limit. The lesson of vanity of all things is taught in deeply buried palaces, in fallen columns, in defaced monuments, in decaying arches, and in crumbling walls;—all perishing under the silent and destructive force of time and the steady action of the elements, in utter mockery of the pride and power of the great people by whom they were called into existence.
    —Autobiography: *Life and Times,* 1881, p. 434

Washington, D.C.
Washington should loom before our mental vision, not merely as an assemblage of magnificent public buildings, and a profusion of fine and fashionable people; not merely as the seat of National power and greatness, not merely as the fortunate place where the nation's great men assemble from year to year to shape the policy, enact the laws, and control the destiny of the republic; not merely as the place where the diplomatic skill and learning of the old world meet and measure

themselves in debate with those of the new, but, as all that, and more. We should contemplate it with much the same feeling with which we contemplate our national flag itself; as the Star Spangled banner, with not one star missing or dimmed, a glorious symbol of civil and religious liberty, expressive of the best ideas and institutions yet devised by the wit of man.

—Speech: "Our National Capital," May 8, 1877, *Douglass Papers*, ser. I, 4:452

In this preeminently deceitful and treacherous atmosphere, promises, even on paper, do not amount to much. Every body is fed and being fed upon great expectations and golden promises, and, since the diet is less than dog cheap, nobody fails of a full supply.

—Speech: "Our National Capital," May 8, 1877, *Douglass Papers*, ser. I, 4:460

The District of Columbia is the one spot where there is no government for the people, of the people and by the people. Its citizens submit to rulers whom they have had no choice in selecting. They obey laws which they had no voice in making. They have a plenty of taxation but no representation. In the great questions of politics in the country they can march with neither army but are relegated to the position of neuters.

—Autobiography: *Life and Times*, 1881, p. 391

Civil Rights
(see also Constitution, Free Speech, Human Rights)

[The Supreme Court in 1883 Civil Rights Cases has effected] a sudden and causeless reversal of all the great rules of legal interpretation by which this Court was governed in other days. . . . It presents the United States before the world as a nation utterly destitute of power to protect the rights of its own citizens upon its own soil.

—Speech: "This Decision Has Humbled the Nation," October 22, 1883, *Douglass Papers*, ser. I, 5:115–16

O for a Supreme Court which shall be as true to the claims of humanity, as the Supreme Court formerly was to the demands of slavery! When that day comes, as come it will, a Civil Rights Bill will not be declared unconstitutional and void, in utter and flagrant disregard of the objects and intentions of the National legislature by which it was enacted, and of the rights plainly secured by the Constitution.

—Speech: "This Decision Has Humbled the Nation," October 22, 1883, Washington, D.C., *Douglass Papers*, ser. I, 5:120

Let us have no country but a free country, liberty for all and chains for none. Let us have one law, one gospel, equal rights for all, and I am sure God's blessing will be upon us and we shall be a prosperous and glorious nation.

—Speech: "Representatives of the Future South," April 12, 1864, *Douglass Papers*, ser. I, 4:31

[R]eversing the action of the Government, defeating the manifest purpose of the Constitution, nullifying the Fourteenth Amendment, and placing itself on the side of prejudice, proscription and persecution.

—Autobiography: *Life and Times*, 1881, p. 395

There is no negro problem. The problem is whether the American people have loyalty enough, honor enough, patriotism enough, to live up to their own constitution.

—Speech: "Colored People's Day at the World Columbian Exposition," August 25, 1893, *Chicago Tribune,* August 26, 1893

Civil War

The contest must now be decide, and decided forever, which of the two, Freedom or Slavery, shall give law to this Republic. Let the conflict come.

—Editorial, *Douglass' Monthly,* March 1861

For this consummation we have watched and wished with fear and trembling. God be praised! that it has come at last.

—Editorial, *Douglass' Monthly,* May 1861

[I]nstead of looking upon the present war as an unmitigated evil, you and I, and all of us, ought to welcome it as a glorious opportunity for imparting wholesome lessons to the southern soul-drivers.

—Editorial: "Revolutions Never Go Backwards," *Frederick Douglass' Paper,* May 5, 1861

The fate of the greatest of all Modern republics trembles in the balance. "To be, or not to be—that is the question." The lesson of the hour is written down in characters of blood and fire. We are taught as with the emphasis of an earthquake, that nations, not less than individuals, are subjects of the moral government of the universe, and that flagrant, long continued, and persistent transgressions of the laws of this Divine government will certainly bring national sorrow, shame, suffering and death. Of all the nations of the world, we seem most in need of this solemn lesson. To-day we have it brought home to our hearths, our homes, and our hearts.

—Speech: "Fighting the Rebels with One Hand," January 14, 1862, *Douglass Papers*, ser. I, 3:474

54th Massachusetts Infantry

If the President is ever to demand justice and humanity, for black soldiers, is this not the time to do it? How many 54ths must be cut to pieces, its mutilated prisoners killed and its living sold into Slavery to be tortured to death before Mr. Lincoln shall say: "Hold, enough!"

—Correspondence: Douglass to Major George L. Stearns, August I, 1863, *Douglass Papers*, ser. 2, 3:270

Another thing is settled, which is that the negro can fight, and will fight. We were accustomed to make him out an excellent Christian, a Christian by nature, a lamb-like animal, smite him once upon one cheek, and he will turn to you the other also; ready to obey, whenever demanded to expose his back to the lash; an Uncle Tom, a religious animal, but it is found out that this animal has a good deal of human nature about it. It is settled by his behavior at Fort Wagner, Port Hudson and Vicksburg, that he will fight.

—Speech: "Black Freedom Is the Prerequisite of Victory," January 13, 1865, *Douglass Papers*, ser. I, 4:56

Massachusetts now welcomes you to arms as soldiers. She has but a small colored population from which to recruit. She has full leave of the general government to send one regiment to the war, and she has undertaken to do it. . . . The day dawns; the morning star is bright upon the horizon! The iron gate of our prison stands half open. One gallant rush from the North will fling it wide open, while four millions of our brothers and sisters shall march out into liberty. The chance is now given you to end in a day the bondage of centuries, and to rise in one bound from social degradation to the plane of common equality with all other varieties of men.

—Autobiography: *Life and Times*, 1881, p. 266

In that terrible battle [Fort Wagner], under the wing of night, more cavils in respect of the quality of negro manhood were set at rest than could have been during a century of ordinary life and observation.

—Autobiography: *Life and Times*, 1881, pp. 267–68

Black Soldiers

We are fighting the Rebels with only one hand when we ought to be fighting them with both. We are recruiting our troops at the north when we out to be recruiting them at the south. We are striking with our white hand, while our black one is chained behind us.

—Speech: "Pictures and Progress," December 3, 1861, *Douglass Papers*, ser. I, 3:466

But one thing I have a right to ask when I am required to march to the battle field, and that is, that I shall have a country or the hope of a country under me, a government that recognizes my manhood around me, and a flag of freedom waving over me!

—Speech: "Pictures and Progress," December 3, 1861, *Douglass Papers*, ser. I, 3:468

We are fighting the rebels with only one hand, when we ought to be fighting them with both. We are recruiting our troops in the towns and villages of the North, when we ought to be recruiting them on the plantations of the South. We are striking the guilty rebels with our soft, white hand, when we should be striking with the iron hand of the black man, which we keep chained behind us.

—Speech: "Fighting the Rebels with One Hand," January 14, 1862, *Douglass Papers*, ser. 3, 3:482–83

I know the colored men of the North; I know the colored men of the South, They are ready to rally under the stars and stripes at the first tap of the drum. Give them a chance; stop calling them "niggers," and call them soldiers. Give them a chance to seek the bubble reputation at the cannon's mouth. Stop telling them they can't fight, and tell them they can fight and shall fight, and they will fight, and fight with vengeance. Give them a chance.

—Speech: "The Proclamation and a Negro Army," February 6, 1863, *Douglass Papers*, ser. I, 3:567

Once let the black man get upon his person the brass letters U.S. let him get an eagle on his button, and a musket on his soldier, and bullets in his pocket, and there is no power on the earth or under the earth which can deny that he has earned the right of citizenship in the United States. I say again, this is our chance, and woe betide us if we fail to embrace it!

—Speech: "Negroes and the National War Effort," July 6, 1863, *Douglass Papers*, ser. 3, 3:596

What business, then have we to fight for the old Union? We are not fighting for it. We are fighting for something incomparably better than the old Union. We are fighting for unity; unity of object, unity of institutions, in which there shall be no North, no South, no East, no West, no black, no white, but a solidarity of the nation, making every slave free, and every free man a voter.

—Speech: "Emancipation, Racism, and the Work before Us," December 4, 1863, *Douglass Papers*, ser. 3, 3:609

While of I course I was deeply pained and saddened by the estimate thus put upon my race, and grieved at the slowness of heart which marked the conduct of the loyal government, I was not discouraged, and urged every man who could to enlist; to get an eagle on his button, a musket on his shoulder, and the star-spangled banner over his head.

—Autobiography: *Life and Times*, 1881, p. 264

Causes

[The] God in history everywhere pronouncing the doom of those nations which frame mischief by law [has caused] a concussion . . . against slavery which would now rock the land.

—Editorial: "The Union and How to Save It," *Douglass' Monthly*, February 1861

There is no geographical reason for national division. Every stream is bridged, and every mountain is tunneled. All our rivers and mountains point to union, not division—to oneness, not to warfare. There is no earthly reason why the corn fields of Pennsylvania should quarrel with the cotton fields of South Carolina. The physical and climatic differences bind them together, instead of putting them asunder.

—Speech: "Fighting the Rebels with One Hand," January 14, 1862, *Douglass Papers*, ser. 3, 3:478

But the sectional character of this war was merely accidental, and its least significant feature. It was a war of ideas, a battle of principles and ideas which united one section and divided the other; a war between the old and new, slavery and freedom, barbarism and civilization; between a government based upon the broadest and grandest declaration of human rights the world ever heard or read, and another pretended government, based upon an open, bold and shocking denial of all rights, except the right of the strongest.

—Speech: There Was a Right Side in the Late War," May 30, 1878, *Douglass Papers*, ser. I, 4:490

Most of the rebellions and uprisings in the history of nations have been for freedom, and not for slavery. They have found their mainspring and power among the lowly. But here was a rebellion, nor for freedom, but for slavery, not to break fetters, but to forge them, not to secure the blessings of liberty, but to bind with chains millions of the human race. It was not from the low, but from the high, not from the plebian, but from the patrician, not from the oppressed, but from the oppressor.

—Speech: "We Must Not Abandon the Observance of Decoration Day," May 30, 1882, *Douglass Papers*, ser. I, 5:47

Confederate Army

The rebel armies fought well, fought bravely, fought desperately, but they fought in fetters. Invisible chains were about them. Deep down in their own consciences there was an accusing voice reminding them that they were fighting for chains and slavery, and not for freedom. They were in chains—entangled with the chains of their own slaves. They not only struggled with our gigantic armies, and with the skill of our veteran generals, but they fought against the moral sense of the nineteenth century—they fought against their own better selves—they fought against the good in their own souls; they were weakened thereby; their weakness was our strength, hence our success.

—Speech: "Sources of Danger to the Republic," February 7, 1867, *Douglass Papers*, ser. I, 4:154–55

It had reached that verge of madness when it had called upon the negro for help to fight against the freedom which he so longed to find, for the bondage he would escape—against Lincoln the emancipator for Davis the enslaver.

—Autobiography: *Life and Times,* 1881, p. 283

Contraband

There must be no calling things by their right names—no going straight to any point which can be reached by a crooked path. When slaves are referred to, they must be called persons held to service or labor. When in the hands of the Federal Government, they are called contrabands— a name that will apply better to a pistol, than to a person.

—Speech: "Fighting the Rebels with One Hand," January 14, 1862, *Douglass Papers,* ser. I, 3:477–78

Costs

The honor of a nation is an important thing. It is said in the Scriptures, "What doth it profit a man if he gain the whole world, and lose his own soul?" It may be said also, "what doth it profit a nation if it gain the whole world, but lose its honor?" I hold that the American Government has taken upon itself the solemn obligation of honor to see that this war, let it be long or let it be short, let it cost much, or let it cost little,—that this war shall not cease until every freedman at the South has the right to vote. It has bound itself to do it.

—Speech: "What the Black Man Wants?" January 26, 1865, *Douglass Papers,* ser. I, 4:66

The late rebellion, undertaken, carried on, [and] persisted in for the sole purpose of establishing and perpetuating a superior class in the United States, intended to make slavery perpetual. It was a rebellion

THE WORDS OF FREDERICK DOUGLASS

that brought misery to a million homes, a rebellion that piled up a debt heavier than a mountain of gold; a rebellion that has filled our streets with stumps of men, mutilated and maimed; that has filled three hundred thousand rough made graves, that aimed to extinguish American liberty utterly.

—Speech: "Govern with Magnanimity and Courage," September 6, 1866, *Douglass Papers*, ser. I, 4:141

Draft

The old cry was raised by the copperhead organs of "an abolition war," and a pretext was thus found for an excuse for refusing to enlist, and for marshaling all the negro prejudice of the North on the rebel side. Men could say they were willing to fight for the Union, but that they were not willing to fight for the freedom of the negroes; and thus it was made difficult to procure enlistments or to enforce the draft.

—Autobiography: *Life and Times*, 1881, p. 278

I had encountered Isaiah Rynders and his gang of ruffians in the old Broadway Tabernacle at our Anti-slavery Society anniversary meeting, and I knew something of the crazy temper of such crowds; but this anti-draft, anti-negro mob, was something more and something worse—it was a part of the rebel force, without the rebel uniform, but with all its deadly hate; it was the fire of the enemy opened in the rear of the loyal army.

—Autobiography: *Life and Times*, 1881, p. 279

Goals

I look at this as an abolition war instead of being a Union war, because I see that the lesser is included in the greater, and that you cannot have the lesser until you have the greater. You cannot have the Union, the Constitution, and republican institutions, until you have stricken down that damning curse, and put it beyond the pale of the Republic. For, while it is in this country, it will make your Union impossible, it will make your Constitution impossible.

—Speech: "Emancipation, Racism, and the Work before Us," December 4, 1863, Philadelphia, *Douglass Papers*, ser. 3, 3:600

The world has witnessed many wars—and history records and perpetuates their memory, but the world has not seen a nobler and grander war than that which the loyal people of this country are now waging against the slaveholding Rebels. The blow we strike is not merely to free a country or continent—but the whole world from Slavery—for when Slavery falls here—it will fall everywhere. We have no business to mourn over our mission. We are writing the statutes of eternal justice and liberty in the blood of the worst of tyrants as a warning to all after-comers. We should rejoice that there was moral life and health enough in us to stand in our appointed place, and do this great service for mankind.

—Speech: "The Mission of the War," January 13, 1864, *Douglass Papers*, ser. 1, 4:6

From the first, I, for one, saw in this war the end of slavery; and truth requires me to say that my interest in the success of the North was largely due to this belief.

—Autobiography: *Life and Times*, 1881, p. 262

Secession
Human governments are neither held together, nor broken up by such mild and gentle persuasives as are implied in the soft phrase—peaceful secession. Theirs is a voice of command, not persuasion. They rest not

upon paper, but upon power. They do not solicit obedience as a favor, but compel it as a duty.

—Editorial: "Dissolution of the Union," *Douglass' Monthly,* January 1861

If there is not wisdom and virtue enough in the land to rid the country of slavery, then the next best thing is to let the South go . . . and be made to drink the wine cup of wrath and fire, which her long career of cruelty, barbarism and blood shall call down upon her guilty head.

—Editorial: "The Union and How to Save It," *Douglass' Monthly,* February 1861

What is a slaveholder but a rebel and a traitor? That is, and must be in the nature of his vocation, his true character. Treason and rebellion are the warp and woof of the relation of master and slave. A man cannot be a slaveholder without being a traitor to humanity and a rebel against the law and government of the ever-living God.

—Speech: "The American Apocalypse," June 16, 1861, *Douglass Papers,* ser. I, 3:440–41

Happily for the cause of human freedom, and for the final unity of the American nation, the South was mad, and would listen to no concessions. They would neither accept the terms offered, nor offer others to be accepted. They had made up their minds that under a given contingency they would secede from the Union and dismember the Republic. That contingency had happened, and they should execute their threat.

—Autobiography: *Life and Times,* 1881, p. 259

This haughty and unreasonable and unreasoning attitude of the imperious South saved the slave and saved the nation. Had the South accepted our concessions and remained in the Union the slave power would in all probability have continued to rule; the north would have become utterly demoralized; the hands on the dial-plate of American civilization would have been reversed, and the slave would have been dragging his hateful chains to-day wherever the American flag floats to the breeze.

—Autobiography: *Life and Times*, 1881, pp. 259–60

Significance

Only mighty forces, resting deep down among the foundations of nature and life, can lash the deep and tranquil sea of humanity into a storm, like that which the world is now witnessing.

—Editorial: "The Wicked Flee When No Man Pursueth," *Douglass' Monthly*, April 1861

It is something to couple one's name with great occasions, and it was a great thing to me to be permitted to bear some humble part in this, the greatest that had thus far come to the American people. It was a great thing to achieve American independence when we numbered three millions, but it was a greater thing to save this country from dismemberment and ruin when it numbered thirty millions.

—Autobiography: *Life and Times*, 1881, p. 254

There was a right side and a wrong side in the late war, which no sentiment ought to cause us to forget, and while to-day we should have malice toward none, and charity toward all, it is no part of our duty to confound right with wrong, or loyalty with treason.

—Speech: There Was a Right Side in the Late War," May 30, 1878, *Douglass Papers*, ser. I, 4:491

Though the doctrine of forgiveness and forgetfulness has been adopted by many of the noblest and most intelligent men of our country, men for whom I have the highest respect, I am wholly unable to accept it, to the extent to which it is asserted, I certainly cannot accept it to the extent of abandoning the observance of Decoration Day. If rebellion was wrong and loyalty right, if slavery was wrong and emancipation right, we are rightfully here today.

—Speech: "We Must Not Abandon the Observance of Decoration Day," May 30, 1882, *Douglass Papers*, ser. I, 5:44

Many disguises have been assumed by the South in regard to that war. It has been said that it was fighting for independence, but the South was already a sharer in the national independence. It has been said that the South was fighting for liberty, but the South was already a sharer in the national liberty. It has been said that the South was fighting for the right to govern itself, but the South has already the ballot and the right to govern itself.

—Speech: "We Must Not Abandon the Observance of Decoration Day," May 30, 1882, *Douglass Papers*, ser. I, 5:46–47

Successful wickedness is contagious and repeats itself. Jefferson Davis and his rebellion successful, would have prepared the way for other rebels and traitors. Instead of our rival and hostile confederacy, in that case, this great country would have in time become divided, torn and rent into numerous petty states, each warring upon and devouring the substance of the other. So this great war of ours may have saved us many wars.

—Speech: "We Must Not Abandon the Observance of Decoration Day," May 30, 1882, *Douglass Papers*, ser. I, 5:48–49

Class

[T]he higher the gradation in intelligence and refinement, the farther removed are all artificial distinctions, and restraints of mere caste or color.

—Autobiography: *Life and Times*, 1881, p. 355

We affect contempt for the castes and aristocracies of the old world and laugh at their assumptions, but at home foster pretensions far less rational and much more ridiculous.

—Autobiography: *Life and Times*, 1881, p. 393

The spirit of caste is malignant and dangerous everywhere. There is the prejudice of the rich against the poor, the pride and prejudice of the idle dandy against the hard handed working man.

—Autobiography: *Life and Times*, 1881, p. 401

Colonization
(see also Abolition)

We see in it a revival of that second enemy of the colored people, the Colonization Society, which, next to slavery, is the deadliest foe to the colored man,—unsettling his plans and improvements, by teaching him to feel that this is not his home; disheartening and subduing his enterprise, by causing him to feel that all effort at self-elevation is in vain; that neither knowledge, temperance, patience, faith, nor virtue, can avail him anything in this land.

—Editorial: "Henry Clay," *North Star*, January 28, 1848

We are of opinion that the *free* colored people generally mean to live in America. . . . Our minds are made up to live here if we can, or die here if we must.

—Editorial: "Colonization," *North Star*, January 26, 1849

We are here . . . and must remain [here] for ever.

—Editorial: "The Destiny of Colored Americans," *North Star*, November 16, 1849

The white and black must fall or flourish together. We shall neither die out, nor be driven out, but we shall go with you, remain with you, and stand either as a testimony against you, or as an evidence in your favor, throughout all your generations.

—Speech: "Henry Clay and Colonization Rant, Sophistry, and Falsehood," February 2, 1851, *Douglass Papers*, ser. I, 2:325

The native land of the American negro is America.

—Speech: "Lessons of the Hour," January 9, 1894, Washington, D.C., *Douglass Papers*, ser. I, 5:598

Colonization is no solution to the race problem. It is an evasion. It is not repenting of wrong butting out of sight the people upon whom wrong has been inflicted.

—Speech: "Lessons of the Hour," January 9, 1894, *Douglass Papers*, ser. I, 5:599

Conscience

Conscience is to the individual soul and to society, what the law of gravitation is to the universe. It holds society together; it is the basis of all trust and confidence; it is the pillar of all moral rectitude. Without it, suspicion would take the place of trust; vice would be more than a match for virtue; men would prey upon each other, like the wild beasts of the desert; and earth would become a *hell*.

—Speech: "Slavery and the Slave Power," December 1, 1850, *Douglass Papers*, ser. I, 2:255–56

Constitution

If the American government has been mean, sordid, mischievous, devilish, it is no proof whatever that the constitution of government has been the same.

—Speech: "The American Constitution and Slavery," March 26, 1860, *Douglass Papers*, ser. I, 3:345

The U.S. Constitution is a written instrument, full and complete in itself. No court, no congress, no legislature, no combination in the country can add one word to it, or take one word from it. It is a thing in itself; complete in itself; has a character of its own. . . . It is a great national enactment, done by the people, and can only be altered, amended, or changed in any way, shape, or form by the people who enacted it.

—Speech: "The American Constitution and Slavery," March 26, 1860, *Douglass Papers*, ser. I, 3:347

It should also be borne in mind that the intentions of those who framed the constitution, be they good or bad, be they for slavery or against slavery, are to be respected so far, and so far only, as they have succeeded in getting these intentions expressed in the written instrument themselves.

—Speech: "The American Constitution and Slavery," March 26, 1860, *Douglass Papers*, ser. I, 3:347

[The] trouble never was in the Constitution, but in the administration of the Constitution. All experience shows that laws are of little value in the hands of those unfriendly to their objects.

—Speech: "This Democratic Conversion Should Not Be Trusted," September 25, 1872, *Douglass Papers*, ser. I, 4:341

Whenever an administration has had the will to do anything, it has generally found constitutional power to do it.

—Speech: "In Law Free; in Fact, a Slave," April 16, 1888, *Douglass Papers*, ser. I, 5:369

Antislavery Intent

We doubt if there were more than a dozen men in the Convention that framed the Constitution who did not expect that slavery in this country would cease forever long before the year 1851. Nor is there anything in the language of the Constitution which casts a shadow of doubt upon this version. There is, to our mind, every reason to believe that the framers of the Constitution intended that it should permanently protect the freedom of every human being in the U.S. The great principle which they laid down as the fundamental objects of the Government and the completeness with which they have excluded every word sanctioning the right of property in man, is no slight testimony in proof of the intention to make the Constitution a permanent liberty document.

—Editorial: "Is the United States Constitution for or against Slavery?" *Frederick Douglass' Paper*, July 24, 1851

Proslavery Intent

To say that the Constitution was intended to uphold Slavery was to assume the framers of the Constitution were the most flagrant knaves ever known, that they were liars and poltroons, keeping the word of promise to the ear and breaking it to the heart. This should not be said without the strongest proofs, and he did not believe such proofs existed. There was not a sentence, nor a syllable in a sentence, of the Constitution, that would lead any one to suppose there was any deceptive intent in it. If that Constitution had dropped down to us from the blue, over-hanging sky, and we had read its contents, there was not a man who could reasonably suppose it was intended to sanction and support the Slave system, but, on the contrary, that everything in it was intended to support justice and equality between man and man.

—Speech: "Is the Plan of the American Union under the Constitution, Anti-Slavery or Not?" May 21, 1857, *Douglass Papers*, ser. I, 3:157

By such a course of thought and reading, I was conducted to the conclusion that the constitution of the United States—inaugurated "to form a more perfect union, establish justice, insure domestic tranquility, provide for the common defense, promote the general welfare, and secure the blessings of liberty"—could not well have been designed at the same time to maintain and perpetuate a system of rapine and murder like slavery; especially, as not one word can be found in the constitution to authorize such a belief.

—Autobiography: *My Bondage and My Freedom,* 1855, p. 229

[C]onstitutions do not execute themselves. We have had justice enough in our Constitution from the beginning to have made slavery impossible. The trouble never was in the Constitution, but in the administration of the Constitution. All experience shows that laws are of little value in the hands of those unfriendly to their objects.

—Speech: "The Democratic Conversion Should Not Be Trusted," September 25, 1872, *Douglass Papers,* ser. I, 4:341

Republican Character

Our republican government is weak only as it touches or partakes of the character of monarchy or an aristocracy or an oligarchy. In its republican features, it is strong. In its despotic features it is weak. Our government, in its ideas, is a government of the people. But unhappily it was framed under conditions unfavorable to purely republican results, it was projected and completed under the influence of institutions quite unfavorable to a pure republican form of government—slavery on the one hand, monarchy on the other.

—Speech: "Sources of Danger to the Republic," February 7, 1867, *Douglass Papers,* ser. I, 4:156–57

Crime

Weeds do not more naturally spring out of a manure pile than crime out of enforced destitution.

—Speech: "Parties Were Made for Men, Not Men for Parties," September 25, 1883, *Douglass Papers,* ser. I, 5:101

If a slave killed his master, or struck down his overseer, or set fire to his master's dwelling, or committed any violence or crime, out of the common way, it was certain to be said that such a crime was the legitimate fruit of the abolition movement.

—Autobiography: *Life and Times,* 1881, p. 69

Death

All is gloom. The grave is at the door. And now, when weighed down by the pains and aches of old age, when the head inclines to the feet, when the beginning and ending of human existence meet, and helpless infancy and painful old age combine together—at this time, this most needful time, the time for the exercise of that tenderness and affection which children only can exercise towards a declining parent—my poor old grandmother, the devoted mother of twelve children, is left all alone, in yonder little hut, before a few dim embers. She stands—she sits—she staggers—she falls—she groans—she dies—and there are none of her children and grandchildren present, to wipe from her wrinkled brow the cold sweat of death, or to place beneath the sod her fallen remains.

—Autobiography: *Narrative,* 1845, pp. 40–41

Sad, indeed, will be the condition of the living, when they fall so low as to cease to venerate the lives and deeds of the noble dead. The virtues brilliantly illustrated by those who go before us, are given as lamps to the feet of aftercoming generations. They light us through the dark, and much entangled wilderness of life. By their hallowed illumination, we may walk with firmer tread, and more courageous faith, through the perils that await us in time.

—Speech: "In Honor of Asa S. Wing," September 11, 1855, *Douglass Papers*, ser. I, 3:109

To have the objects of our earnest love caught away from us forever, to see the majestic pillars of our strength and trust falling all around us, to watch with eager eyes the flickering lamps of our best and fondest hopes one by one, as in solemn procession, going out in darkness, will sometimes make even the strong man to quiver with a sense of his loneliness and his nothingness. The powers above and around him seem too much for him. He is hemmed in on every hand, and to himself he appears but as the small dust of the balance, at the mercy of every breeze.

—Speech: "Eulogy of William Jay," May 12, 1859, *Douglass Papers*, ser. I, 3:250

Happy and glorious is the lot of that man, when standing at the verge of the grave, winding up his affairs in this life, surveying the whole course of his career on earth, who can truthfully say, in full view of the past, and the great incoming future, I have no regrets for the uses to which I have put my time and talents.

—Speech: "Eulogy of William Jay," May 12, 1859, *Douglass Papers*, ser. I, 3:257

I am not of that sentimental school of moralists who think it right to speak only of the virtues of the dead. The power exerted by some men after death is far greater than in life, and it frequently happens that to expose the faults of departed great men, is a much higher and more commanding duty than to extol their virtues. Wrong and injustice to the living are remarkably disposed to conceal themselves from the light of truth, under the overshadowing examples of the great among the dead.

—Speech: "Eulogy of William Jay," May 12, 1859, *Douglass Papers*, ser. I, 3:275

As we walk under the light of this glorious orb, never thinking of any possible speck upon its surface, but thanking God for the brilliant illumination, so let us accept gratefully the shining example of the late honorable WM. JAY. He has taught us the great purposes of life. He has taught us how to live; he has taught us how to die.

—Speech: "Eulogy of William Jay," May 12, 1859, *Douglass Papers*, ser. I, 3:276

At such a time, and in such a place, when a man is about closing his eyes on this world and ready to step into the eternal unknown, no word of reproach or bitterness should reach him or fall from his lips; and on this occasion there was to this rule no transgression on either side.

—Autobiography: *Life and Times*, 1881, pp. 345–46

When one has advanced far in the journey of life, when he has seen and traveled over much of this great world, and has had many and strange experience of shadow and sunshine, when long distances of time and space have come between him and his of departure, it is natural that his thoughts should return to the place of his beginning, and that he should be seized with a strong desire to revisit the scenes of his early recollection, and live over in memory the incidents of his childhood.

—Autobiography: *Life and Times*, 1881, p. 348

The time is at hand when the last American slave, and the last American slaveholder will disappear behind the curtain which separates the living from the dead, and when neither master nor slave will be left to tell the story of their respective relations, and what happened in those relations to either.

—Autobiography: *Life and Times*, 1881, p. 372

There was no true man in the land who did not share the pain of the illustrious sufferer while he lingered in life, or who could refuse a tear when the final hour came when his life and suffering ended.

—Autobiography: *Life and Times*, 1881, p. 386

Declaration of Independence
(*see also Fourth of July*)

I have said that the Declaration of Independence is the RING-BOLT to the chain of your nation's destiny, so, indeed, I regard it. The principles, contained in that instrument are saving principles. Stand by those principles, be true to them on all occasions, in all places, against all foes, and at whatever cost.

—Speech: "What to the Slave Is the Fourth of July?" July 5, 1852, *Douglass Papers*, ser. I, 2:363–64

Your fathers have said that man's right to liberty is self-evident. There is no need of argument to make it clear. The voices of nature, of conscience, of reason, and of revelation, proclaim it as the right of all rights, the foundation of all trust, and of all the responsibility. Man was born with it. It was his before he comprehended it. The *deed* conveying it to him is written in the center of his soul, and is recorded in Heaven. The sun in the sky is not more palpable to the sight than man's right to liberty is to the moral vision.

—Speech: "The Dred Scott Decision," May 1857, *Douglass Papers,* ser. I, 3:168

Disagreement

A difference of opinion, like a discord in music, sometimes gives the highest effects of harmony.

—Speech: "Who and What Is Woman?" May 24, 1886, *Douglass Papers,* ser. I, 5:261

Diversity
(see also Assimilation, Immigration)

We are made up of a variety of nations—Chinese, Jews, Africans, Europeans, and all sorts. These different races give the Government a powerful arm to defend it. They will vie with each other in hardship and peril, and will be united in defending it from all its enemies, whether from within or without.

—Speech: "At Last, at Last, the Black Man Has a Future," April 22, 1870, *Douglass Papers,* ser. I, 4:272

I want a home here not only for the negro, the mulatto and the Latin races, but I want the Asiatic to find a home here in the United States, and feel at home here, both for his sake and for ours. Right wrongs no man. If respect is had to majorities, the fact that only one-fifth of the population of the globe is white and the other four-fifths are colored, ought to have some weight and influence in disposing of this and similar questions.

—Speech: "Our Composite Nationality," December 7, 1869, *Douglass Papers,* ser. I, 4:252

Education

No nation can now shut itself up from the surrounding world, and trot round in the same old path of its fathers without interference. The time was when such could be done. Long established customs of hurtful character could formerly fence themselves in, and do their evil work with social impunity. Knowledge was then confined and enjoyed by the privileged few, and the multitude walked on in mental darkness. But a change has now come over the affairs of mankind. Walled cities and empires have become unfashionable. The arm of commerce has borne away the gates of the strong city. Intelligence is penetrating the darkest corners of the globe. Oceans no longer divide, but link nations together.

—Speech: "What to the Slave Is the Fourth of July?" July 5, 1852, *Douglass Papers,* ser. I, 2:387

[N]o one class or variety of people can furnish them [domestic and menial labor] exclusively without degradation.

—Editorial: "The Plan for the Industrial School," *Frederick Douglass' Paper,* March 24, 1854

The true antidote . . . for *black slaves,* is an enlightened body of black freemen.

—Editorial: "The Kansas-Nebraska Bill," *Frederick Douglass' Paper,* September 15, 1854

The reading of these speeches [in Caleb Bingham's *Columbian Orator* (1821)] . . . enabled me to give tongue to many interesting thoughts, which had frequently flashed away for want of utterance.

—Autobiography: *My Bondage and My Freedom*, 1855, p. 91

From the cradle to the grave, the oldest and the wisest, not less than the youngest and the simplest, are but learners; and those who learn most, seem to have most to learn.

—Speech: "The Trials and Triumphs of Self-Made Men," January 4, 1860, *Douglass Papers*, ser. I, 3:291

We must educate ourselves. Let us resolve to point the finger of scorn at every colored man who refuses to send his children to school. You will find that the more intelligent and refined you become, the more your white brethren will respect you.

—Speech: "A Friendly Word to Maryland," November 17, 1864, *Douglass Papers*, ser. I, 4:50.

It is not enough [that blacks] can read books which white men have written, or solve problems by rules which white men have laid down— we must not only be receivers of light, but givers as well. [If blacks] will continue to strut about in the mental "old clothes" of the white race and refuse to think for themselves they will be a disgraced race. They should not only sing the White man's Hymns, but be able to make Hymns of their own.

—Editorial: "A Year at the Era," *New National Era*, August 24, 1871

The common school is the basis of our whole system, and without it the United States would be little better than uneducated Haiti.

—Speech: "Schools Are a Common Platform of Nationality," May 9, 1872, *Douglass Papers*, ser. I, 4:301

Education, the sheet anchor of safety to society where liberty and justice are secure, is a dangerous thing to society in the presence of injustice and oppression.

—Speech: "We Are Confronted by a New Administration," April 16, 1885, *Douglass Papers*, ser. I, 5:188

But if man is without education although with all his latent possibility attaching to him he is, as I have said, but a pitiable object; a giant in body but a pigmy in intellect, and at best but half a man. Without education he lives within the narrow, dark and grimy walls of ignorance. He is a poor prisoner without hope.

—Speech: "The Blessings of Liberty and Education," September 3, 1894, *Douglass Papers*, ser. I, 5:623

To deny education to any people is one of the greatest crimes against human nature. It is easy to deny them the means of freedom and the rightful pursuit of happiness and to defeat the very end of their being.

—Speech: "The Blessings of Liberty and Education," September 3, 1894, *Douglass Papers*, ser. I, 5:623

Slavery

Slavery was a poor school for acquiring moral, religious, or intellectual improvement. He had never had the advantage of attending a day school, and all that he knew of literature had been obtained by stealth, for in the country whence he came, it was considered a crime against law to teach a slave to read; and there the colored child was not even allowed to learn to spell the name of the God who made him.

—Speech: "The Cambria Riot, My Slave Experience, and My Irish Mission," December 5, 1845, *Douglass Papers*, ser. I, 1:87

To educate a man is to unfit him to be a slave.
—Autobiography: *Narrative*, 1845, p. 31

That which to him was a great evil, to be carefully shunned, was to me a great good, to be diligently sought; and the argument which he so warmly urged, against my learning to read, only served to inspire me with a desire and determination to learn.
—Autobiography: *Narrative*, 1845, p. 32

The more I read, the more I was led to abhor and detest my enslavers. I could regard them in no other light than a band of successful robbers, who had left their homes, and gone to Africa, and stolen us from our homes, and in a strange land reduced us to slavery.
—Autobiography: *Narrative*, 1845, p. 35

I was broken in body, soul, and spirit. My natural elasticity was crushed, my intellect languished, the disposition to read departed, the cheerful spark that lingered about my eye died; the dark night of slavery closed in upon me; and behold a man transformed into a brute!
—Autobiography: *Narrative*, 1845, p. 49

Vocational

What I thought of as best was rather a series of workshops, where colored people could learn some of the handicrafts, learn to work in iron, wood, and leather, and where a plain English education could also be taught. I argued that the want of money was the root of all evil to the colored people. They were shut out from all lucrative employments and compelled to be merely barbers, waiters, coachmen and the like at wages so low that they could lay up little or nothing. Their poverty kept them ignorant and their ignorance kept them degraded.

We needed more to learn how to make a good living than to learn Latin and Greek.

—Autobiography: *Life and Times*, 1881, pp. 221–22

Emancipation
(see also Abolition, Slavery)

My answer to the question, What shall be done with the four million slaves if emancipated? shall be alike short and simple: Do nothing with them, but leave them just as you have left other men, to do with and for themselves. . . . Let us alone. Do nothing with us, for us, or by us as a particular class. What you have done with us thus far has only worked to our disadvantage. We now simply ask to be allowed to do for ourselves.

—Speech: "The Black Man's Future in the Southern States," February 5, 1862, *Douglass Papers*, ser. 3, 3:499

What a glorious day when Slavery shall be no more in this Country, when we have blotted out this system of wrong, and made this United States in fact and in truth what it is in theory—The land of the Free and the Home of the Brave.

—Speech: "The Proclamation and a Negro Army," February 6, 1863, *Douglass Papers*, ser. 3, 3:569

Law and the sword can and will in the end abolish slavery, [but they could not so soon abolish] the malignant slaveholding sentiment which has kept the slave system alive in this country during two centuries. . . . The slave having ceased to be the abject slave of a single master, his enemies will endeavor to make him the slave of [white] society at large.

—Speech: "Emancipation, Racism, and the Work before Us,"
December 4, 1863, *Douglass Papers*, ser. I, 3:599–600

Whence came the abolition of slavery? To me the result is no
miracle. . . . I contemplate the termination of slavery simply as a natural and logical event. . . . A natural and prolific breeder of pride, selfishness, and love of power, it perished at the hands of its own progeny.

—Speech: "We Are Not Yet Quite Free," August 3, 1869, *Douglass
Papers*, ser. I, 4:230

The world has never seen any people turned loose to such destitution as were the four million slaves of the South. . . . They were free,
without roofs to cover them, or bread to eat, or land to cultivate, and
as a consequence died in such numbers as to awaken the hope of their
enemies that they would soon disappear.

—Speech: "Celebrating the Past, Anticipating the Future," April 14,
1875, *Douglass Papers*, ser. I, 4:413

What shall we do with the Negro? Do nothing with us! Your doing
with us has already played the mischief with us. Do nothing with us!
If . . . the Negro cannot stand on his own legs, let him fall. . . . All I ask
is, give him a chance to stand on his own legs! let him alone! . . . give
him fair play and let him alone, but *be sure you give him fair play.*

—Speech: "Let the Negro Alone," May 11, 1865, *Douglass Papers*,
ser. I, 4:202

Whence came the abolition of slavery? The theologian says, God.
The politician says, Lincoln. The abolitionist says, Garrison. The
statesman says, war. To me the result is no miracle. I am not skilled
in tracing the action of supernatural agencies; hence I contemplate
the termination of slavery simply as a natural and logical event. The

evil contained the seeds of its own destruction. A natural and pro-lific breeder of pride, selfishness, and love of power, it perished at the hand of its own progeny. The world might have permitted slav-ery a good while longer, but for the pride and ambition of its vota-ries. Mr. Garrison would not abolish it. Mr. Lincoln did not wish to interfere with it. The Republican party did not seek it. The armies of the Union with their generals, were opposed to its abolition. All parties were quite willing to let it alone within its own limits. But its own inborn arrogance and violence would not permit it to live any longer.

—Speech: We Are Not Yet Quite Free," August 3, 1869, *Douglass Papers*, ser. I, 4:230–31

They resented his emancipation as an act of hostility toward them, and, since they could not punish the emancipator, they felt like pun-ishing the object which that act had emancipated.

—Autobiography: *Life and Times*, 1881, p. 295

The abolition of slavery has not merely emancipated the negro, but liberated the whites. . . .

—Autobiography: *Life and Times*, 1881, p. 353

The school of the negro since leaving slavery has not been much of an improvement on his former condition. Individuals of the race have here and there enjoyed large benefits from emancipation, and the result is seen in their conduct, but the mass have had their liberty coupled with hardships which tend strongly to keep them a dwarfed and miserable race.

—Speech: "Strong to Suffer, and Yet Strong to Strive," April 16, 1886, *Douglass Papers*, ser. I, 5:230

Emancipation Proclamation

We are all liberated by this proclamation. It is a mighty event for the bondman, but it is still a mightier event for the nation at large.

—Speech: "The Proclamation and a Negro Army," February 6, 1863, *Douglass Papers*, ser. I, 3:550

It was the first gray streak of morning after a long and troubled night of all abounding horrors.

—Speech: "Freedom Has Brought Duties," January 1, 1883, *Douglass Papers*, ser. I, 5:57

The effect of the proclamation abroad was highly beneficial to the loyal cause. Disinterested parties could now see in it a benevolent character. It was no longer a mere strife for territory and dominion, but a contest of civilization against barbarism.

—Autobiography: *Life and Times*, 1881, p. 277

The time for argument was passed. It was not logic, but the trump of jubilee, which everybody wanted to hear. We were waiting and listening as for a bolt from the sky, which should rend the fetters of four millions of slaves; we were watching, as it were, by the dim light of the stars, for the dawn of a new day; we were longing for the answer to the agonizing prayers of centuries.

—Autobiography: *Life and Times*, 1881, p. 276

For my own part, I took the proclamation, first and last, for a little more than it purported; and saw in its spirit, a life and power far beyond its letter. Its meaning to me was the entire abolition of slavery, wherever the evil could be reached by the Federal arm, and I saw that its moral power would extend much further. It was in my estimation an immense gain to have the war for the Union committed to the extinction of Slavery, even from a military necessity.

—Autobiography: *Life and Times,* 1881, p. 277

Emigration
(see also Colonization)

The business of this nation is to protect its citizens where they are, not to transport them where they will not need protection.

—Speech: "The Negro Exodus from the Gulf States," September 12, 1879, *Douglass Papers,* ser. I, 4:526

While necessity often compels men to migrate; to leave their old homes and seek new ones; to sever old ties and create new ones; to do this the necessity should be obvious and imperative. It should be a last resort and only adopted after carefully considering what is against the measure as well as what is in favor of it. There are prodigal sons everywhere, who are ready to demand the portion of goods that would fall to them and betake themselves to a strange country. Something is ever lost in the process of migration, and much is sacrificed at home for what is gained abroad.

—Speech: "The Negro Exodus from the Gulf States," September 12, 1879, *Douglass Papers,* ser. I, 4:526–27

The habit of roaming from place to place in pursuit of better conditions of existence is by no means a good one. A man should never leave his home for a new one till he has earnestly endeavored to make his immediate surroundings accord with his wishes. The time and energy expended in wandering from place to place, if employed in making him comfortable where he is, will, in nine cases out of ten, prove the best investment. No people ever did much for themselves or for the world, without the sense and inspiration of native land; of a fixed home; of a familiar neighborhood, and common associations.

—Speech: "The Negro Exodus from the Gulf States," September 12, 1879, *Douglass Papers*, ser. I, 4:527

Land is not worth much where there are no people to occupy it, and a mule is not worth much where there is no one to use it.

—Speech: "The Negro Exodus from the Gulf States," September 12, 1879, *Douglass Papers*, ser. I, 4:527

Not only is the South the best locality for the negro on the ground of his political powers and possibilities, but it is best for him as a field of labor. He is there, as he is nowhere else, an absolute necessity. He has a monopoly of the labor market. His labor is the only labor which can successfully offer itself for sale in that market. This, with a little wisdom and firmness, will enable him to sell his labor there on terms more favorable to himself than he can elsewhere. As there are no competitors or substitutes, he can demand living prices with the certainty that the demand will be complied with. Exodus would deprive him of this advantage.

—Speech: "The Negro Exodus from the Gulf States," September 12, 1879, *Douglass Papers*, ser. I, 4:530

The deserving hired man gets his wages increased when he can tell his employer that he can get better wages elsewhere. And when all hope is gone from the hearts of the laboring-class of the old world, they can come across the sea to the new. If they could not do that their crushed hearts would break under increasing burdens. The right to emigrate is one of the most useful and precious of all rights.

—Speech: "The Negro Exodus from the Gulf States," September 12, 1879, *Douglass Papers*, ser. I, 4:531

It would seem that education and emigration go together with us, for as soon as a man rises amongst us, capable, by his genius and learning, to do us great service, just so soon he finds that he can serve himself better by going elsewhere.

—Autobiography: *Life and Times*, 1881, p. 223

There is little reason to hope that any considerable number of the free colored people will ever be induced to leave this country, even if such a thing were desirable. The black man (*un*like the Indian) loves civilization. He does not make very great progress in civilization himself but he likes to be in the midst of it, and prefers to share its most galling evils, to encountering barbarism.

—Autobiography: *Life and Times*, 1881, p. 224

There is too much moving about. The man who succeeds anywhere stays there. Every time the shiftless moves he carries his old self with him, and with that old self he can do no better in one country than another. This is our home. Let us stay here.

—Speech: "Boyhood in Baltimore," September 6, 1891, *Douglass Papers*, ser. I, 5:484

Employment

Let the colored man therefore, put forth the energies of his mind, lay aside his menial occupations, endeavor to assume the same elevated position occupied by his white neighbor, and soon will he obtain that respect which ever belongs to the employment of intellect in its legitimate and proper sphere. Let him leave the grog shops and taverns, and no longer stand idling at the corners of the streets, but go out into the world, and devote his hands and his mind to some useful and honorable occupation.

—Speech: "Advice to My Canadian Brothers and Sisters," August 3, 1854, *Douglass Papers*, ser. I, 2:530

Prejudice against the free colored people in the United States has shown itself nowhere so invincible as among mechanics. The farmer and the professional man cherish no feeling so bitter as that cherished by these. The latter would starve us out of the country entirely. At this moment I can more easily get my son into a lawyer's office to study law than I can into a blacksmith's shop to blow the bellows and to wield the sledge-hammer. Denied the means of learning useful trades we are pressed into the narrowest limits to obtain a livelihood. In times past we have been the hewers of wood and drawers of water for American society, and we once enjoyed a monopoly in menial employments, but this is so no longer. Even these employments are rapidly passing away out of our hands. The fact is (every day begins with the lesson, and ends with the lesson) that colored men must learn trades; must find new employments; new modes of usefulness to society, or that they must decay under the pressing wants to which their condition is rapidly bringing them.

—Autobiography: *Life and Times*, 1881, p. 225

We must become mechanics; we must build as well as live in houses; we must make as well as use furniture; we must construct bridges as well as pass over them, before we can properly live or be respected by our fellow men. We need mechanics as well as ministers. We need workers in iron, clay, and leather. We have orators, authors, and other professional men, but these reach only a certain class, and get respect for our race in certain select circles. To live here as we ought we must faster ourselves to our countrymen through their every-day cardinal wants. We must not only be able to *black* boots, but *make* them.

—Autobiography: *Life and Times*, 1881, p. 225

Evolution

I do not know that I am an evolutionist, but to this extent I am one. I certainly have more patience with those who trace mankind upward from a low condition, even from the lower animals, then with those that start him at a high point of perfection and conduct him to a level with the brutes. I have no sympathy with a theory that starts man in *heaven* and stops him in hell.

—Speech: "It Moves," November 20, 1883, *Douglass Papers*, ser. I, 5:129

Family

I have an industrious and neat companion and four dear children. These dear children are ours—not to work up into rice, sugar and tobacco, but to train them in the paths of wisdom and virtue. Oh! sir, a slaveholder never appears to me so completely an agent of hell, as when I think of the look upon my dear children.

—Correspondence: Douglass to Thomas Auld, September 8, 1848, *Douglass Papers*, ser. 3, 1:313.

The family is the fountain head of all mental and moral influence.

—Speech: "Pictures and Progress," December 3, 1861, *Douglass Papers*, ser. I, 3:454

Fathers

The whisper that my master was my father, may or may not be true; and, true or false, it is of but little consequence to my purpose whilst the fact remains, in all its glaring odiousness, that slaveholders have ordained, and by law established, that the children of slave women shall in all cases follow the condition of their mothers; and this is done too obviously to administer to their own lusts, and make a gratification of their wicked desires profitable as well as pleasurable; for by this cunning arrangement, the slaveholder, in cases not a few, sustains to his slaves the double relation of master and father. . . . The master is frequently compelled to sell this class of his slaves, out of deference to the feelings of his white wife; and, cruel as the deed may strike anyone to be, for a man to sell his own children to human flesh-mongers, it is often the dictate of humanity for him to do so, for, unless he does this, he must not only whip them himself, but must stand by and see one white son tie up his brother, of but few shades darker complexion than himself, and ply the gory lash to his back; and if he lisp one word of disapproval, it is set down to his parental partiality, and only makes a bad matter worse, both for himself and the slave whom he would protect and defend.

—Autobiography: *Narrative,* 1845, pp. 14–15

Genealogical trees do not flourish among slaves. A person of some consequence here in the north, sometimes designated father, is literally abolished in slave law and slave practice.

—Autobiography: *My Bondage and My Freedom,* 1855, p. 22

Firsts

The mind of man has a special attraction towards first objects. It delights in the dim and shadowy outlines of the coming fact. There is a calm and quiet satisfaction in the contemplation of present attainments; but the great future, and the yet unattained, awaken in the soul the deepest springs of poetry and enthusiasm.

—Speech: "The Douglass Institute," September 29, 1865, *Douglass Papers*, ser. I, 4:88

Fourth of July
(see also Declaration of Independence, Patriotism)

I am not included within the pale of this glorious anniversary! Your high independence only reveals the immeasurable distance between us. The blessings in which you, this day rejoice, are not enjoyed in common. The rich inheritance of justice, liberty, prosperity and independence, bequeathed by your fathers, is shared by you, not by me. The sunlight that brought life and healing to you, had brought stripes and death to me. This Fourth [of] July is *yours,* not *mine. You* may rejoice, *I* must mourn. To drag a man in fetters into the great illuminated temple of liberty, and call upon him to join you in glorious anthem, were inhuman mockery and sacrilegious irony. Do you men, citizen, to mock me, by asking me to speak to-day?

—Speech: "What to the Slave Is the Fourth of July?" July 5, 1852, *Douglass Papers*, ser. I, 2:368

Standing, there, identified with the American bondman, making his wrongs mine, I do not hesitate to declare, with all my soul, that the character and conduct of this nation never looked blacker to me than on this 4th of July! Whether we turn to the declarations of the past, or to the professions of the present, the conduct of the nation seems equally hideous and revolting. America is false to the past, false to the present, and solemnly binds herself to be false to the future. Standing with God and the crushed and bleeding slave on this occasion, I will, in the name of humanity which is outraged, in the name of liberty which is fettered, in the name of the constitution and the Bible, which are disregarded and trampled upon, dare to call in question and to denounce, with all of the emphasis I can command, everything that serves to perpetuate slavery—the great sin and shame of America!

—Speech: "What to the Slave Is the Fourth of July?" July 5, 1852, *Douglass Papers,* ser. I, 2:368–69

What, to the American slave, is your 4th of July? I answer: a day that reveals to him, more than all other days in the year, the gross injustice and cruelty to which he is the constant victim. To him, your celebration is a sham; your boasted liberty, an unholy license; your national greatness, swelling vanity; your sounds of rejoicing are empty and heartless; your denunciations of tyrants, brass fronted impudence; your shouts of liberty and equality, hollow mockery; your prayers and hymns, your sermons and thanksgivings, will all of your religious parade, and solemnity, are, to him, mere bombast, fraud, deception, impiety, and hypocrisy—a thin veil to cover up crimes which would disgrace a nation of savages. There is not a nation on the earth guilty of practices, more shocking and bloody, than are the people of these United States, at this very hour.

—Speech: "What to the Slave Is the Fourth of July?" July 5, 1852, *Douglass Papers,* ser. I, 2:371

France

The French people are naturally a temperate people. They are economical in all things, except in the matter of display. They eat without gluttony, drink without drunkenness, and amuse themselves at very little expense of time and money.

—Speech: "My Foreign Travels," December 15, 1887, *Douglass Papers*, ser. I, 5:297

Free Blacks

In the Northern States, a fugitive slave, liable to be hunted at any moment like a felon, and to be hurled into the terrible jaws of slavery—doomed by an inveterate prejudice against color to insult and outrage on every hand, (Massachusetts out of the question)— denied the privileges and courtesies common to others in the use of the most humble means of conveyance—shut out from the cabins on steamboats—refused admission to respectable hotels—caricatures, scorned, scoffed, mocked and maltreated with impunity by any one, (no matter how black his heart,) so he has a white skin.

—Correspondence: Douglass to William Lloyd Garrison, January I, 1846, Douglass *Papers*, ser. 3, 1:74

When sober men take the advice of drunkards; when honest men seek the admonition of thieves; and when men of veracity put themselves under the instruction of liars; it will then be time enough for *me* to take counsel of slaveholders and negro-haters respecting the best method for our advancement and improvement.

—Speech: "Henry Clay and Colonization Rant, Sophistry, and Falsehood," February 2, 1851, *Douglass Papers*, ser. I, 2:324

I assert then that *poverty, ignorance, and degradation* are the combined evils; or in other words, these constitute the social disease of the free colored people of the United States. To deliver them from this triple malady, is to improve and elevate them, by which I mean simply to put them on an equal footing with their white fellow countrymen in the sacred right to *"Life, Liberty,* and the pursuit of happiness."

—Correspondence: Douglass to Harriet Beecher Stowe, March 8, 1853, *Douglass Papers,* ser. 2, 3:222

The most telling, the most killing refutation of slavery is the presentation of an industrious, enterprising, thrifty, and intelligent free black population.

—Autobiography: *Life and Times,* 1881, p. 226

The hostility between the whites and blacks of the South is easily explained. It has its root and sap in the relation of slavery, and was incited on both sides by the cunning of the slave masters. Those masters secured their ascendency over both the poor whites and blacks by putting enmity between them.

—Correspondence: Douglass et al. to Andrew Johnson, February 7, 1866, *Douglass Papers,* ser. 1, 4:612.

Free Speech

This right of speech is very dear to the hearts of intelligent lovers of liberty. It is the delight of the lovers of liberty, it is the dread and terror of tyrants.

—Speech: "Agitate, Agitate," October 14, 1852, *Douglass Papers,* ser. 1, 2:415

There can be no right of speech where any man, however lifted up, or however humble, however young, or however old, is overawed by force, and compelled to suppress his honest sentiments. Equally clear is the right to hear. To suppress free speech is a double wrong. It violates the rights of the hearer as well as those of the speaker. It is just as criminal to rob a man of his right to speak and hear as it would be to rob him of his money.

—Speech: "A Plea for Freedom of Speech in Boston," December 9, 1860, *Douglass Papers*, ser. I, 2:423

No right was deemed by the fathers of the Government more sacred than the right of speech. It was in their eyes, as in the eyes of all thoughtful men, the great moral renovator of society and government. Daniel Webster called it a home-bred right, a fireside privilege. Liberty is meaningless where the right to utter one's thoughts and opinions has ceased to exist. That, of all rights, is the dread of tyrants. It is the right which they first of all strike down. They know its power. Thrones, dominions, principalities, and powers, founded in injustice and wrong are sure to tremble if men are allowed to reason of righteousness, temperance and of a judgment to come in their presence.

—Speech: "A Plea for Freedom of Speech in Boston," December 9, 1860, *Douglass Papers*, ser. I, 3:422

To suppress free speech is a double wrong. It violates the rights of the hearer as well as those of the speaker. It is just as criminal to rob a man of his right to speak and hear, as it would be to rob him of his money. . . . When a man is allowed to speak because he is rich and powerful it aggravates the crime of denying the right to the poor and humble.

—Speech: "A Plea for Freedom of Speech in Boston," December 9, 1860, *Douglass Papers*, ser. I, 3:423

Freedom
(see also Abolition, Slavery, Slaves)

I often found myself regretting my own existence, and wished myself dead; and but for the hope of being free, I have no doubt but that

I should have killed myself, or done something for which I should have been killed.
—Autobiography: *Narrative*, 1845, p. 36

It was this everlasting thinking of my condition that tormented me. There was no getting rid of it. It was pressed upon me by every object within sight or hearing, animate or inanimate. The silver trump of freedom had roused my soul to eternal wakefulness. Freedom now appeared, to disappear no more forever. It was hear in every sound, and seen in every thing. It was ever present to torment me with a sense of my wretched condition. I saw nothing without seeing it, I heard nothing without hearing it, and felt nothing without feeling it. It looked from every star, It smiled in every calm, breathed in every wind, and moved in every storm.
—Autobiography: *Narrative*, 1845, p. 36

Our house stood within a few rods of the Chesapeake Bay, whose broad bosom was ever white with sails from every quarter of the habitable globe. Those beautiful vessels robed in purest white, so delightful to the eye of freemen, were to me so many shrouded ghosts, to terrify and torment me with thoughts of my wretched condition.
—Autobiography: *Narrative*, 1845, p. 49

You are loosed from your moorings, and are free; I am fast in my chains, and am a slave! You move merrily before the gentle gale, and I sadly before the bloody whip! You are freedom's swift-winged angels, that fly round the world; I am confined in bands of iron!
—Autobiography: *Narrative*, 1845, p. 49

My long crushed spirit rose, cowardice departed, bold defiance took its place; and I now resolved that, however long I might remain a slave in form, the day had passed forever when I could be a slave in fact.

I did not hesitate to let it be known of me, that the white man who expected to succeed in whipping, must also succeed in killing me.

 —Autobiography: *Narrative,* 1845, p. 54

We had talked long enough; we were now ready to move; if not now, we never should be; and if we did not intend to move now, we had as well fold our arms, sit down, and acknowledge ourselves fit only to be slaves.

 —Autobiography: *Narrative,* 1845, p. 63

I felt as one might imagine the unarmed mariner to feel when he is rescued by a friendly man-of-war from the pursuit of a pirate.

 —Autobiography: *Narrative,* 1845, p. 74

Life is not lightly regarded by men of sane minds. It is precious, alike to the pauper and to the prince—to the slave, and to his master; and yet, I believe there was not one among us, who would not rather have been shot down, than pass away life in hopeless bondage.

 —Autobiography: *My Bondage and My Freedom,* 1855, p. 162

The more you make men free, the more freedom is strengthened, and the more men you give an interest in the welfare and safety of the State, the greater is the security of the State.

 —Speech: "A Friendly Word to Maryland," November 17, 1864, *Douglass Papers,* ser. I, 4:48

Freedman's Savings and Trust Bank
(*see also Prosperity*)

It seemed fitting to me to cast in my lot with my brother freedmen, and help to build up an institution which represented their thrift and economy to so striking advantage; for the more millions accumulated there, I thought, the more consideration and respect would be shown to the colored people of the whole country.

—Autobiography: *Life and Times,* 1881, pp. 314–15

I could not help reflecting on the contrast between Frederick the slave boy, running about at Col. Lloyd's with only a tow linen shirt to cover him, and Frederick—President of a bank counting its assets by millions. I had heard of golden dreams, but such dreams had no comparison with this reality.

—Autobiography: *Life and Times,* 1881, p. 315

The fact is, and all investigation shows it, that I was married to a corpse. The fine building was there with its marble counters and black walnut finishings, the affable and agile clerks, and the discreet and comely colored cashier; but the LIFE, which was the money, was gone, and I found that I had been placed there with the hope that by "some drugs, some charms, some conjuration, or some mighty magic," I would bring it back.

—Autobiography: *Life and Times,* 1881, pp. 317–18

Friendship

The term friend is a delightful one, filled with a thousand sweet harmonies. In journeying through this vale of tears, life is desolate indeed, if unblest by friendship. A friend is a very precious gift. A brother is not always a friend—a sister is not always a friend, and even a wife may not always be a friend, nor a husband a friend. The central idea of friendship, and the main pillar of it is *"trust."* Where there is no *trust,* there is no friendship. We cannot love those whom we cannot trust. The basis of all *trust* is truth. There cannot be trust—lasting trust—where the truth is not. Men must be true in each other, or they cannot trust each other.

—Speech: "Trust, the Basis of Charity," January 4, 1853, *Douglass Papers*, ser. I, 2:452

Fugitive Slaves

"Trust no man!" I saw in every white man an enemy, and in almost every colored man cause for distrust. It was a most painful situation; and, to understand it, one must needs experience it, or imagine himself in similar circumstances. Let him be a fugitive slave in a strange land—a land given up to be the hunting-ground for slaveholders—whose inhabitants are legalized kidnappers—where he is every moment subjected to the terrible liability of being seized upon by his fellow-men, as the hideous crocodile seizes upon his prey!

—Autobiography: *Narrative*, 1845, p. 75

Among honest men an honest man will well be content with one name, and to acknowledge it at all times and in all places; but toward fugitives, Americans are not honest.

—Autobiography: *My Bondage and My Freedom*, 1855, p. 197

Fugitive Slave Law of 1850

In glaring violation of justice, in shameless disregard of the forms of administering law, in cunning arrangement to entrap the defenseless, and in diabolical intent, this Fugitive Slave Law stands alone in the annals of tyrannical legislation. I doubt if there be another nation on the globe, having the brass and baseness to put such a law on the statute-book.

—Speech: "What to the Slave Is the Fourth of July?" July 5, 1852, *Douglass Papers*, ser. I, 2:376

The True Remedy for the Fugitive Slave Bill [was a] good revolver, a steady hand, and a determination to shoot down any man attempting to kidnap.

—Editorial "The True Remedy for the Fugitive Slave," *Frederick Douglass' Paper*, June 9, 1854

I could take no step in it without exposing myself to fine and imprisonment, for these were the penalties imposed by the fugitive slave law, for feeding, harboring, or otherwise assisting a slave to escape from his master; but in face of this fact, I can say, I never did more congenial, attractive, fascinating, and satisfactory work. True, as a means of destroying slavery, it was like an attempt to bail out the ocean with a teaspoon, but the thought that there was *one* less slave, and one more freeman,—having myself been a slave, and a fugitive slave—brought to my heart unspeakable joy.

—Autobiography: *Life and Times*, 1881, 208

Government
(see also Constitution, Law, Politics)

[N]ations seldom listen to advice from individuals, however reasonable. They are taught less by theories than by facts and events.

—Autobiography: *Life and Times*, 1881, pp. 262–63

Checks and Balance System

But it is said that we must have a check some where. We are great on checks. We must have some checks against these fanatical majorities, and we have recently been told that majorities can be as destructive and more arbitrary than individual despots, especially when the individuals are humble. "Uriah Heeps." If this be so; if this is the truth, I think that we ought to part with republican government at once. If it be true that one man is more likely to be wiser, or is likely to be wiser than the majority—that one man is likely to wield the government more entirely [in] the interest of the people than will a majority, if one man is a safer guide for the people than nearly two-thirds of the best representatives—if that be true, let us have a one man government at once, let us have done with republicanism—let us try the experiment of the one man government.

—Speech: "Sources of Danger to the Republic," February 7, 1867, *Douglass Papers,* ser. 1, 4:165

Citizenship

[The Supreme Court's] impractical doctrine of two citizenships [effectively means] no citizenship. The one destroys the other. . . . The true doctrine is one nation, one country, one citizenship and one law for all the people.

—Correspondence: Douglass to Gerrit Smith, July 3, 1874, in Philip S. Foner, *The Life and Writings of Frederick Douglass,* 5 vols. (New York: International Publishers, 1950–75), 4:306

Congress

A very brief acquaintance will convince one that Congress is not the place for either a vain man or a weak man. He may be a very great man at home and a very small man in Congress. It is one thing to be weighed and measured by ones friends, neighbors, and admirers, but quite another thing to be measured in comparison with the chosen representatives of forty millions of people. In this presence your weak man will easily sink toward nothingness, and your vain man, if not hopelessly blind and insensible, will have his vanity completely taken out of him. The floors, the gallery, the streets even, are all against him. He will be allowed to pass in a crowd, but will find no admitting eyes feasted upon his fine face, his fine figure or his fine clothing. The people there gathered are accustomed to hear and see great men. They are experts, they know at a glance the genuine from the spurious, the false from the true, the sheet iron thunder of this stage from the royal thunder of heaven.

—Speech: "Our National Capital," May 8, 1877, *Douglass Papers*, ser. I, 4:470

Democracy

No people can be much respected in this country, where all are eligible to hold office, that cannot point to any one of their class in an honorable, responsible position. In sending a few men to Congress, the negroes of the South have done much to dispel prejudice and raise themselves in the estimation of the country and the world.

—Speech: "The Negro Exodus from the Gulf States," September 12, 1879, *Douglass Papers*, ser. I, 4:528

A nation composed of all classes should be governed by no one class exclusively. All should be included, and none excluded. Thus aggrieved classes would be rendered impossible.

—Speech: "Our Destiny Is Largely in Our Own Hands," April 16, 1883, *Douglass Papers*, ser. I, 5:68

We hold it to be self-evident that no class or color should be the exclusive rulers of this country. If there is such a ruling class, there must of course be a subject class, and when this condition is once established this Government of the people, by the people and for the people, will have perished from the earth.

—Speech: "Parties Were Made for Men, Not Men for Parties," September 25, 1883, *Douglass Papers*, ser. I, 5:100

No man can be said to represent another, who has not been chosen by that other to represent him.

—Speech: "Who and What Is Woman?" May 24, 1886, *Douglass Papers*, ser. I, 5:255

Expansionism

When the slave power bore rule, and a spirit of injustice and oppression animated and controlled every part of our government, I was for limiting our dominion to the smallest possible margin; but since liberty and equality have become the law of our land, I am for extending our dominion whenever and wherever such extension can peaceably and honorably, and with the approval and desire of all the parties concerned, be accomplished.

—Autobiography: *Life and Times*, 1881, p. 320

While slavery existed I was opposed to all schemes for the extension of American power and influence. But since its abolition I have gone with him who goes farthest for such extension.

—Autobiography: *Life and Times*, 1881, p. 444

Foreign Aid

It might be important to know what San Domingo could do for us, but it is a vastly nobler inquiry to ask what we could do for San Domingo.

—Editorial, *New National Era*, April 20, 1871

Majority Rule

We have recently been told that majorities can be as destructive and more arbitrary than individual despots. . . . If this be so . . . I think that we ought to part with Republican government at once.

—Speech: "Sources of Danger to the Republic," February 7 1867, *Douglass Papers*, ser. I, 4:164–65

I believe majorities can be despotic and have been arbitrary, but arbitrary to whom? Arbitrary when arbitrary at all, always to unrepresented classes. What is the remedy? A consistent republic in which there shall be no unrepresented classes. For when all classes are represented the rights of all classes will be respected.

—Speech: "Sources of Danger to the Republic," February 7, 1867, *Douglass Papers*, ser. I, 4:165

[W]hen you want good government go to the mass.

—Speech: "Women's Rights Are Not Inconsistent with Negro Rights," November 19, 1868, *Douglass Papers*, ser. I, 4:184

Individuals may be very great, but the masses of men are greater. The great heart of the people may be mistaken, but it is always honest and disinterested.

—Speech: "William the Silent," February 8, 1869, *Douglass Papers*, ser. I, 4:197

Political Office

An appointment to any important and lucrative office under the United States government, usually brings its recipient a large measure of praise and congratulation on the one hand, and much abuse and disparagement on the other; and he may think himself singularly fortunate if the censure does not exceed the praise.

—Autobiography: *Life and Times*, 1881, p. 328

[O]nly one person can be appointed to any one office, only one can be pleased, while many are offended; unhappily, resentment follows disappointment, and this resentment often finds expression in disparagement and abuse of the successful man.

—Autobiography: *Life and Times*, 1881, p. 328

My cause first, midst, last and always, whether in office or out of office, was and is that of the black man; not because he is black, but because he is a man, and a man subjected in this country to peculiar wrongs and hardships.

—Autobiography: *Life and Times*, 1881, p. 387

Presidency

By the Constitution of the United States our King reigns over us for the term of four years. It seems a short term; but experience shows that it is quite long enough for the perpetuation of almost innumerable mischiefs, and to thwart and defeat the most beneficent measures. Our King is armed with mighty powers, the veto power among them. He is Commander-in-Chief of the army and navy. During his reign he can exercise his power as rigorously as any of the crowned heads of Europe, and do so with greater impunity. I assert fearlessly, that while Americans are ever boasting of the sovereignty of the people, there is no Government on the earth which can be administered in more open violation of the principles of freedom, or in more flagrant contempt for the rights and wishes of the people, than the American Government during a Presidential term.

—Speech: "Slavery and the Irrepressible Conflict," August 1, 1860, *Douglass Papers*, ser. I, 3:373

When your President is elected, once familiarly seated in the national saddle, his feet in the stirrups, his hand on the reins, he can drive the national animal almost where he will. He can administer this government with contempt for public opinion, for the opinions and wishes of the people, such as no crowned head in Europe imitates toward his subjects.

—Speech: "Sources of Danger to the Republic," February 7, 1867, *Douglass Papers*, ser. I, 4:160–61

[The Presidential veto] has no business in our Constitution. It is alien to every idea of republican government—borrowed from the old world, from king craft and priest craft, and all other adverse craft to republican government. It is anti-republican, anti-democratic, anti-common sense. It is based upon the idea, the absurdity, that one man is more than many men—that one man separate from the people by his exalted station—one man sitting apart from the people in his room, surrounded by his friends, his cliques, his satellites, will be likely to bring to the consideration of public measures, a higher wisdom, a larger knowledge, a purer patriotism, than will the representatives of the republic in the face and in the presence of the multitude with the flaming sword of the press waving over them, directly responsible to their constituents, immediately in communication with the great heart of the people—that one man will be likely to govern more wisely than will a majority of the people.

—Speech: "Sources of Danger to the Republic," February 7, 1867, *Douglass Papers*, ser. I, 4:164

Purpose

[The true object of government is] to see that all have an equal chance in the race of life.

—Speech: "In Law Free; in Fact, a Slave," April 16, 1888, *Douglass Papers*, ser. I, 5:369

The true object for which governments are ordained among men is to protect the weak against the encroachments of the strong, to hold its strong arm of justice over all the civil relations of its citizens and to see that all have an equal chance in the race of life. Now, in the case of the negro citizen. Our national government does precisely the reverse of all this. Instead of protecting the weak against the encroachments of the strong, it tacitly protects the strong in its encroachments upon the weak.

—Speech: "In Law Free; in Fact, a Slave," April 16, 1888, *Douglass Papers*, ser. I, 5:369

Supreme Court

[Re: Dred Scot Decision, 1857] Happily for them, human rights were decided in a higher court than the Supreme Court of the United States. The Supreme Court of the United States is high, but the Supreme Court of God is higher. It cannot undo what God Almighty has done, he has made all men free, and had made their freedom self-evident. Some of the good people of this country laughed at Seward when he spoke of the higher law; but Seward was not the first to speak of that higher law—Lord Brougham had spoken of it long before. The very moment that God said "let us make a man in our own image," that moment freedom became inherent in man.

—Speech: "Colored Men's Rights in This Republic," May 14, 1857, *Douglass Papers*, ser. I, 3:147

[The Supreme Court is] the autocratic point in our National Government. No monarch in Europe has a power more absolute. . . . [What] His Holiness, the Pope, is to the Roman Catholic Church, the Supreme Court is to the American State.

—Speech: "This Decision Has Humbled the Nation," October 22, 1893, *Douglass Papers*, ser. I, 5:115.

Great Britain
(see also Emancipation, Ireland)

I want to say a word about John Bull. I have a peculiar affection for Englishmen, and a respect for the English character. They were among the first to do us injury and the first to try to right the injury.

—Speech: "Slavery, the Slumbering Volcano," April 23, 1848, *Douglass Papers*, ser. I, 2:163

Great Britain bowing down, confessing and forsaking her sins—her sins against the weak and despised—is a spectacle which nations present but seldom. No achievements in arts or arms, in letters or laws, can equal this. And the world owes Britain more for this example of humility and honest repentance than for all her other contributions to the world's progress.

—Speech: "The Significance of Emancipation in the West Indies," August 3, 1857, *Douglass Papers*, ser. I, 3:194

England is to-day reaping the bitter consequences of her own injustice and oppression. Ask any man of intelligence, "What is the chief source of England's weakness? What has reduced her to the rank of a second-class power?" and if truly answered, the answer will be

"Ireland!" But poor, ragged, hungry, starving and oppressed as Ireland is, she is strong enough to be a standing menace to the power and glory of England.

—Autobiography: *Life and Times*, 1881, p. 401

Haiti

History will be searched in vain for a warrior, more humane, more free from the spirit of revenge, more disposed to protect his enemies, and less disposed to practice retaliation for acts of cruelty than General Toussaint L'Ouverture.

—Speech: "Haiti among the Foremost Civilized Nations of the Earth," January 2, 1893, *Douglass Papers*, ser. 1, 5:507

[The] revolutionary spirit of Haiti is her curse, her crime, her greatest calamity and the explanation of the limited condition of her civilization.

—Speech: "Haiti and the Haitian People," January 2, 1893, *Douglass Papers*, ser. 1, 5:514–18

Speaking for the Negro, I can say, we owe much to Walker for his Appeal; to John Brown for the blow struck at Harpers Ferry; to Lundy and Garrison for their advocacy, and to the abolitionists in all the countries of the world. . . . [B]ut we owe incomparably more to Haiti than to them all. I regard her as the original pioneer emancipator of the nineteenth century.

—Speech: "Haiti and the Haitian People," January 2, 1893, *Douglass Papers*, ser. 1, 5:528

Even if it were true that a white man could, by reason of his alleged superiority, gain something extra from the servility of Haiti, it would be the height of meanness for a great a nation like the United States to take advantage of such servility on the part of a weak nation. The American people are too great to be small, and they should ask nothing of Haiti on grounds less just and reasonable than those upon which they would ask anything of France or England.

—Autobiography: *Life and Times*, 1881, p. 443

The mission of Haiti was to dispel this degradation and dangerous delusion, and to give to the world a new and true revelation of the black man's character. This mission, she has performed and performed it well.

—Speech: "Haiti and the Haitian People," January 2, 1893, *Douglass Papers*, ser. I, 5:529

Harpers Ferry
(see also Civil War)

But it was said that John Brown invaded a peaceable community, and had with others raised the standard of civil war; and this was an act of gross treason. He had to say, in answer to this, that John Brown did not invade a peaceful neighbourhood or community. What was slavery? A standing insurrection from beginning to end—a perpetual chronic insurrection. Every slaveholder in America was an insurrectionist, the 350,000 slaveholders, with the American Government so-called at their back, were but an armed band of insurgents against the just rights and liberties of their fellow-men. John Brown merely stepped in to interrupt and arrest this insurrection against the rights and liberties of mankind; and he did right.

—Speech: "John Brown and the Slaveholders' Insurrection," January 30, 1860, *Douglass Papers*, ser. I, 3:317

When John Brown proclaimed emancipation to the slaves of Maryland and Virginia he added to his war power the force of a moral earthquake. Virginia felt all her strong-ribbed mountains to shake under the heavy thread of armed insurgents. Of his army of nineteen her conscience made an army of nineteen hundred.

—Speech: "Did John Brown Fail?" May 30, 1881, *Douglass Papers*, ser. I, 5:17

Until this blow was struck, the prospect for freedom was dim, shadowy and uncertain. The irrepressible conflict was one of words, votes and compromises. When John Brown stretched forth his arm the sky was cleared. The time for compromise was gone—the armed hosts of freedom stood face to face over the chasm of a broken Union—and the clash of arms was at hand. The South staked all upon getting possession of the Federal Government, and failing to do that, drew the sword of rebellion and thus made her own, and not John Brown's the lost cause of the century.

—Speech: "Did John Brown Fail?" May 30, 1881, *Douglass Papers*, ser. I, 5:35

History

We have to do with the past only as we can make it useful to the present and to the future. To all inspiring motives, to noble deeds which can be gained from the past, we are welcome. But now is the time, the important time. Your fathers have lived, died, and have done their work, and have done much of it well. You live and must die, and you must do your work. You have no right to enjoy a child's share in the labors of your fathers, unless your children are to be blest by your labors. You have no right to wear out and waste the hard-earned fame of your fathers to cover your indolence.

—Speech: "What to the Slave Is the Fourth of July?" July 5, 1852, *Douglass Papers*, ser. I, 2:366

The ability to make future generations debtors for our knowledge and experience, and their ability to appreciate and improve upon it, as the result of the same, is one of the grandest perfections of mankind.

—Speech: "Great Britain's Example Is High, Noble, and Grand," August 6, 1885, *Douglass Papers*, ser. I, 5:201

Home

To have a home, the Negro must have a Country, and he is an enemy to the moral progress of the Negro, whether he knows it or not, who calls upon him to break up his home in this country, for an uncertain home in Africa.

—Speech: "Lessons of the Hour," January 9, 1894, *Douglass Papers*, ser. I, 5:597

Every man who thinks at all must know that home is the fountain head, the inspiration, the foundation and the main support, not only of all social virtue but of all motives to human progress, and that no people can prosper, or amount to much, unless they have a home, or the hope of a home. A man who has no such an object . . . is a nobody and will never be anything else.

—Speech: "Lessons of the Hour," January 9, 1894, *Douglass Papers*, ser. I, 5:598

Humanity

[T]hough I am more closely connected and identified with one class of outraged, oppressed and enslaved people, I cannot allow myself to be insensible to the wrongs and sufferings of any part of the great family of man.

—Correspondence: Douglass to William Lloyd Garrison, February 26, 1846, *Douglass Papers*, ser. 3, 1:94

I know the cause of humanity is one the world over. He who really and truly feels for the American slave, cannot steel his heart to the woes of others; and he who thinks himself an abolitionist, yet cannot enter into the wrongs of others, has yet to find a true foundation for his anti-slavery faith.

—Correspondence: Douglass to William Lloyd Garrison, February 26, 1846, *Douglass Papers*, ser. 3, 1:96

I may be asked, why I am so anxious to bring this subject before the British public—why I do not confine my efforts to the United States. My answer is, first, that slavery is the commonest enemy of mankind, and all mankind should be made acquainted with its abominable character. My next answer is, that the slave is a man, and, as such, is entitled to your sympathy as a brother. All the feelings, all the susceptibilities, all the capacities, which you have, he has. He is a part of the human family. He has been the prey—the common prey—of Christendom for the last 300 years, and is but right, it is but just, it is but proper, that his wrongs should be known throughout the world.

—Speech: "American Slavery, American Religion, and the Free Church of Scotland," May 22, 1846, *Douglass Papers*, ser. 1, 1:292

A man, without force, is without the essential dignity of humanity. Human nature is so constituted, that it cannot honor a helpless man, although it can pity him; and even this it cannot do long, if the signs of power do not rise.

—Autobiography: *My Bondage and My Freedom*, 1855, p. 141

The thought of being a creature of the *present* and the *past*, troubled me, and I long to have a *future*—a future with hope in it. To be shut up entirely to the past and present, is abhorrent to the human mind; it is to the soul—whose life and happiness is unceasing progress—what the prison is to the body; a blight and mildew, a hell of horrors.

—Autobiography: *My Bondage and My Freedom*, 1855, pp. 155–56

Man is distinguished from all other animals, by the possession of certain definite facilities and powers, as well as by physical organization and proportions. He is the only two-handed animal on the earth—the only one that laughs, and nearly the only one that weeps. . . . His speech, his reason, his power to acquire and to retain knowledge . . . his hopes, his fears, his aspirations, his prophecies . . . his good and his bad, his innocence and his guilt, his joys and his sorrows proclaim [the Negro's] manhood in speech that all mankind practically and readily understand.

—Speech: "The Claims of the Negro Ethnologically Considered," July 12, 1854, *Douglass Papers*, ser. I, 2:502

A single human being was of more interest than all else on earth.

—Speech: "The Trials and Triumphs of Self-Made Men," January 4, 1860, *Douglass Papers*, ser. I, 3:292

Races and varieties of the human family appear and disappear, but humanity remains and will remain forever.

—Speech: "Our Composite Nationality," December 7, 1869, *Douglass Papers*, ser. I, 4:245

The whole of humanity . . . is ever greater than a part. Men only know themselves by knowing others, and contact is essential to this knowledge. . . . all are needed to temper, modify, round, and complete the whole man and the whole nation.

—Speech: "Our Composite Nationality," December 7, 1869, *Douglass Papers*, ser. I, 4:254–55

Human nature is proud and perverse among the low as well as among the high. A man must be low indeed when he does not want some one below him. If he cannot have an Irishman, he wants a negro; and if he cannot have a negro to command, he would like to have a dog! Anything to be above something; but just now these unhappy people see nothing solid below themselves, and consequently, do not know to what the world is coming.

—Speech: "Our National Capital," May 8, 1877, *Douglass Papers*, ser. I, 4:460

I am not a violent advocate of the doctrine of the total depravity of human nature. I am inclined, on the whole, to believe it a tolerably good nature, yet instances do occur which oblige me to concede that men can and do act from mere personal and selfish motives.

—Autobiography: *Life and Times*, 1881, p. 316

Believing, as I firmly do believe, that human nature, as a whole, contains more good than evil, I am willing to trust the whole, rather than a part, in the conduct of human affairs.

—Speech: "Who and What Is Woman?" May 24, 1886, *Douglass Papers*, ser. I, 5:256

[The types of mankind] differ like the waves, but are one like the sea.

—Speech: "A Sentimental Visit to England," September 22, 1887, *Douglass Papers*, ser. I, 5:267

In the East as in the West; in Egypt as in America; in all the world human nature is the same. Conditions may vary but the nature of man is permanent.

—Speech: "My Foreign Travels," December 15, 1887, *Douglass Papers*, ser. I, 5:328

Human Rights
(see also Capital Punishment, Civil Rights)

I am a Democrat in the largest sense of the word—a friend of equal rights, and I believe that I live in a nation which has nothing to do whatever with the graduation of human rights.

—Speech: "The 1848 Revolution in France," April 27, 1848, *Douglass Papers*, ser. I, 2:115

Human rights stand upon a common basis; and by all the reason that they are supported, maintained and defended, for one variety of the human family, they are supported, maintained and defended for *all* the human family; because all mankind have the same wants, arising out of a common nature. A diverse origin does not disprove a common nature, nor does it disprove a united destiny. The essential characteristics of humanity are everywhere the same.

—Speech: "The Claims of the Negro Ethnologically Considered," July 12, 1854, *Douglass Papers*, ser. I, 2:523–24

There are such things in the world as human rights. They rest upon no conventional foundation, but are eternal, universal and indestructible.

—Speech: "Our Composite Nationality," December 7, 1869, *Douglass Papers*, ser. I, 4:250

I know of no rights to race superior to the rights of humanity, and when there is a supposed conflict between human and national rights, it is safe to go the side of humanity.

—Speech: "Our Composite Nationality," December 7, 1869, *Douglass Papers*, ser. I, 4:250

Man is man the world over. This fact is affirmed and admitted to any effort to deny it. The sentiments we exhibit, whether love or hate, confidence or fear, respect or contempt, will always imply a like humanity. A smile or a tear has no nationality. Joy and sorrow speak alike in all nations, and they above all the confusion of tongues proclaim the brotherhood of man.

—Speech: "Our Composite Nationality," December 7, 1869, *Douglass Papers*, ser. I, 4:257

Humor

I have been greatly helped to bear up under unfriendly conditions, too, by a constitutional tendency to see the funny sides of things, which has enabled me to laugh at follies that others would soberly resent.

—Autobiography: *Life and Times*, 1881, p. 362

Immigration
(see also Assimilation, Diversity)

The same mighty forces which have swept to our shores the overflowing populations of Europe; which have reduced the people of Ireland three millions below its normal standard; will operate in a similar manner upon the hungry population of China and other parts of Asia. Home has its charms, and native land has its charms, but hunger, oppression and destitution will dissolve these charms and send men in search of new countries and new homes.

—Speech: "Our Composite Nationality," December 7, 1869, *Douglass Papers*, ser. I, 4:247–48

The Chinese in themselves have first rate recommendations. They are industrious, docile, cleanly, frugal; they are dexterous of hand, patient in toil, marvelously gifted in the power of imitation, and have but few wants.

—Speech: "Our Composite Nationality," December 7, 1869, *Douglass Papers*, ser. I, 4:249

If we would reach a degree of civilization higher than any yet attained, we should welcome to our ample continent all nations, kindreds, tongues and peoples, and as fast as they learn our language and comprehend the duties of citizenship, we should incorporate them into the American body politic. The outspread wings of the American eagle are broad enough to shelter all who are likely to come.

—Speech: "Our Composite Nationality," December 7, 1869, *Douglass Papers*, ser. I, 4:256

Nativism

If the white race may exclude all other races from this continent, it may rightfully do the same in respect to all other lands . . . and thus have all the world to itself. . . . I hold that a liberal and brotherly welcome to all who are likely to come to the United States is the only wise policy which this nation can adopt.

—Speech: "Our Composite Nationality," December 7, 1869, *Douglass Papers*, ser. I, 4:253

Repugnance to the presence and influence of foreigners is an ancient feeling among men. It is peculiar to no particular race or nation. It is met with, not only in the conduct of one nation towards another, but in the conduct of the inhabitants of the different parts of the same country, some times of the same city, and even of the same village.

—Speech: "Our Composite Nationality," December 7, 1869, *Douglass Papers*, ser. I, 4:250

My sympathies are not limited to my relation to any race. I can take no part in oppressing and persecuting any variety of the human family. Whether in Russia, Germany or California, my sympathy is with the oppressed, be he Chinaman or Hebrew.

—Speech: "We Must Not Abandon the Observance of Decoration Day," May 30, 1882, *Douglass Papers*, ser. I, 5:51

Individuality

I believe in individuality, but individuals are, to the mass, like waves to the ocean. The highest order of genius is as dependent as is the lowest. It, like the loftiest waves of the sea, derives its power and greatness from the grandeur and vastness of the ocean of which it forms a part. We differ as the waves, but are one as the sea.

—Speech: "Self-Made Men," March 1893, *Douglass Papers*, ser. I, 5:549

Inertia

Men will long travel the old road, though you show them a shorter and better one, simply because they have always travelled that road.

—Speech: "It Moves," November 20, 1883, *Douglass Papers*, ser. I, 5:135–36

Evils, multitudinous and powerful, avail themselves of routine, custom and habit, and manage to live on, long after their baleful influence is well-known and felt.

—Speech: "It Moves," November 20, 1883, *Douglass Papers*, ser. I, 5:136

Innocence

Innocence, you know, lives in the sunlight—it rushes out into the day—it asks to be examined, and searched, and tried. This is its language. You never hear it crying "Rocks, cover us; and Mountains, on us fall, and hide us from the face of Truth and Justice!" This is the language of guilt—of those convinced of their own iniquity. Innocence never bolts and bars its meeting house doors, to shut out the light, nor hides itself behind some "important engagement." It never does any such things as this. It rushed forth to be seen. Its element is the light. It opens its own eyes and is willing to be seen. Its element is the light. It opens its own eyes and is willing to have the eyes of the world opened on itself. It is glorious, and I love it. The nature of guilt was never set more clearly in a few words than by the Blessed Redeemer, when he said, that "it hateth the light, neither cometh to the light, lest its deeds be revealed." Eighteen hundred years ago, as it is now, was the reason of this obvious—because God looks on sin with no degree of allowance; and truth will not hold that man guiltless who, in the light of the nineteenth century, upholds American Slavery, in any shape or form whatever.

—Speech: "Baptists, Congregationalists, the Free Church, and Slavery," December 23, 1845, *Douglass Papers*, ser. I, 1:105

[I]nnocence needs no defense until it is accused.
   —Autobiography: *Life and Times*, 1881, p. 442

Ireland
(see also Great Britain)

Instead of a democratic government, I am under a monarchical government [in Ireland]. Instead of the bright blue sky of America, I am covered with the soft grey fog of the Emerald Isle. I breathe, and lo! the chattel becomes a man. I gaze around in vain for one who will question my equal humanity, claim me as his slave, or offer me an insult. I employ a cab—I am seated beside white people—I reach the hotel—I enter the same door—I am shown into the same parlor—I dine at the same table—and no one is offended. No delicate nose grows deformed in my presence. I find no difficulty here in gaining admission into any place of worship, instruction or amusement, on equal terms with people as white as any I ever saw in the United States. I meet nothing to remind me of my complexion. I find myself regarded and treated at every turn with the kindness and deference paid to white people.
   —Correspondence: Douglass to William Lloyd Garrison, January 1, 1846, *Douglass Papers*, ser. 3, 1:74–75

It was once said by [Daniel] O'Connell, that the history of the Irish people might be traced, like a wounded man through the crowd, by the blood.

—Speech: "Persecution on Account of Faith, Persecution on Account of Blood," January 26, 1851, *Douglass Papers*, ser. I, 2:291

The Irish people, warm hearted, generous, and sympathizing with the oppressed everywhere when they stand upon their own green island, are instantly taught on arriving in this Christian country to hate and despise the colored people. They are taught to believe that we eat the bread which of right belongs to them. The cruel lie is told the Irish that our adversity is essential to their prosperity. Sir, the Irish American will find out his mistake one day. He will find that in assuming our avocation he has also assumed our degradation. But for the present we are sufferers.

—Speech: "A Nation in the Midst of a Nation," May 11, 1853, *Douglass Papers*, ser. I, 2:433

The Irishman educated, is a model gentleman; the Irishman ignorant and degraded, compares in form and feature with the negro!

—Speech: "The Claims of the Negro Ethnologically Considered," July 12, 1854, *Douglass Papers*, ser. I, 2:520

I hardly need say, That I am in sympathy with Home Rule for Ireland, as held by Mr. Gladstone, I am so, both for the sake of England and for the sake of Ireland. The former will throw off a tremendous load both in money and in reputation by granting it. The glory of England will cease to be soiled with shame for the grievances of Ireland, and Ireland will be put upon her good behavior before the world.

—Speech: "A Sentimental Visit to England," September 22, 1887, *Douglass Papers*, ser. I, 5:269

Justice
(see also Law)

Justice is often painted with bandaged eyes. She is described in forensic eloquence, as utterly blind to wealthy or poverty, high or low, white or black, but a mask of iron, however thick, could never blind American justice, when a black man happens to be on trial. Here, even more than elsewhere, he will find all presumptions of law and evidence against him.

—Speech: "Our Destiny Is Largely in Our Own Hands," April 16, 1883, *Douglass Papers*, ser. I, 5:63

The lesson of all the ages on this point is, that a wrong done to one man is a wrong done to all men. It may not be felt at the moment, and the evil day may be long delayed, but so sure as there is a moral government of the universe, so sure will the harvest of evil come.

—Speech: "This Decision Has Humbled the Nation," October 22, 1883, *Douglass Papers*, ser. I, 5:117

Where justice is denied, where poverty is enforced, where ignorance prevails, and where any one class is made to feel that society is an organized conspiracy to oppress, rob and degrade them, neither persons nor property will be safe.

—Speech: "Strong to Suffer, and Yet Strong to Strive," April 16, 1886, *Douglass Papers*, ser. I, 5:229

Woman should have justice as well as praise, and if she is to dispense with either, she can better afford to part with the latter than the former.

—Speech: "Speech at the 1848 Women's Rights Convention at Seneca Falls," in Philip S. Foner, *Frederick Douglass on Women's Rights* (Westport, Conn., Greenwood Press, 1976), 59

Labor

(see also Class, Slavery)

Abolition

Your determination to strictly adhere to the principle of equality in compensating agents is good. I would not consent to work side by side with a Br[other] agent paying the same for the necessaries [of] life—laboring as hard as myself and yet for his labor getting less than myself. Nor could I on the other hand be satisfied—with a reversed arrangement by which I should have less than equal fellow laborer.

—Correspondence: Douglass to Wendell Phillips, February 10, 1844, *Douglass Papers*, ser. 3, 1:16

Economic Exploitation

This sharp contrast of wealth and poverty, as every thoughtful man knows, can exist only in one way, and from one cause, and that is by one getting more than its proper share of the reward of industry, and the other side getting less—and that in some way labor has been defrauded or otherwise denied of its due proportion, and we think that the facts, as well as this philosophy, will support this view in the present case, and do so conclusively. We utterly deny that the colored people of the South are too lazy to work, or that they are indifferent to their physical wants; as already said, they are the workers of that section.

—Speech: "Parties Were Made for Men, Not Men for Parties," September 25, 1883, *Douglass Papers*, ser. 1, 5:99

Southern

Besides being dependent upon the roughest and flintiest kind of labor, the climate of the South makes such labor uninviting and harshly repulsive to the white man. He dreads it, shrinks from it, and refuses it. He shuns the burning sun of the fields and seeks the shade of the verandas.

—Autobiography: *Life and Times*, 1881, p. 337

Neither natural, artificial, nor traditional causes stand in the way of the freedman to labor in the South. Neither the heat nor the fever-demon which lurks in her tangled and oozy swamps affrights him, and he stands to-day the admitted author of whatever prosperity, beauty, and civilization are now possessed by the South, and the admitted arbiter of her destiny.

—Autobiography: *Life and Times*, 1881, p. 337

His labor made him a slave, and his labor can, if he will, make him free, comfortable, and independent. It is more to him than fire, swords, ballot-boxes, or bayonets. It touches the heart of the South through its pocket.

—Autobiography: *Life and Times*, 1881, p. 338

Not even to gratify its own anger and resentment could it afford to allow its fields to go uncultivated, and its tables unsupplied with food. Hence the freedman, less from humanity than cupidity, less from choice than necessity, was speedily called back to labor and life.

—Autobiography: *Life and Times*, 1881, p. 338

Unions

What labor everywhere wants, what it ought to have and will some day demand and receive, is an honest day's pay for an honest day's work. As the laborer becomes more intelligent he will develop what capital already possess—that is the power to organize and combine for its own protection. Experience demonstrates that there may be a slavery of wages only a little less galling and crushing in its effects than chattel slavery, and that this slavery of wages must go down with the other.

—Speech: "Parties Were Made for Men, Not Men for Parties," September 25, 1883, *Douglass Papers,* ser. I, 5:96

A strike for higher wages is seldom successful and is often injurious to the strikers; the losses sustained are seldom compensated by the concessions gained.

—Speech: "Parties Were Made for Men, Not Men for Parties," September 25, 1883, *Douglass Papers,* ser. I, 5:99

White Workers

The slaveholders, with craftiness peculiar to themselves, by encouraging the enmity of the poor, laboring white men against the blacks, succeeds in making the said white man almost as much a slave as the black slave himself.

—Autobiography: *My Bondage and My Freedom,* 1855, p. 177

Law
(see also Constitution, Crime)

A wise man has said that few people are found better than their laws, but many have been found worse; and the American people are no exception to this rule.

—Speech: "The American Constitution and Slavery," March 26, 1860, *Douglass Papers,* ser. I, 3:349

Law is not merely an arbitrary enactment with regard to justice, reason, or humanity; . . . [it] is in its nature opposed to wrong.

—Editorial: "The Constitution of the United States: Is It Pro-Slavery or Anti-Slavery?" *Frederick Douglass' Paper,* March 26, 1860

[Laws] against fundamental morality are not binding upon anybody.

—Editorial: "Is It Right and Wise to Kill a Kidnapper?" *Frederick Douglass' Paper*, June 9, 1854

A great man once said it was useless to re-enact the laws of God, meaning thereby the laws of Nature. But a greater man than he will yet teach the world that it is useless to re-enact any other laws with any hope of their permanence.

—Speech: "The Proclamation and a Negro Army," February 6, 1863, *Douglass Papers*, ser. 3, 3:555

The first duty of a government is to make its laws respected, and this can only be done by their lust and impartial administration. A law which is applied in one way to one class and in another way to another class and is not applied at all to a third class, must sooner or later lose its majesty and fall into general contempt.

—Interview: "One Country, One Law, One Liberty for All Citizens," January 1889, *Douglass Papers*, ser. I, 5:401

Liberty
(see also Declaration of Independence, Slavery)

No man can be truly free whose liberty is dependent upon the thought, feeling, and action of others; and who has himself no means in his own hands for guarding, protecting, defending, and maintaining that liberty.

—Autobiography: *Life and Times*, 1881, p. 295

In coming to a fixed determination to run away, we did more than Patrick Henry, when he resolved upon liberty or death. With us it was a doubtful liberty at most, and almost certain death if we failed. For my part, I should prefer death to hopeless bondage.

—Autobiography: *Narrative*, 1845, p. 62

Lies

Falsehood is ever most dangerous when it most resembles truth.

—Speech: "Henry Clay and Colonization Rant, Sophistry, and Falsehood," February 2, 1851, *Douglass Papers*, ser. I, 2:313

When I was a younger man than now . . . I thought it my duty to contradict all the falsehoods told in respect to my conduct; but I soon found that if I did so I would have little time to do anything else. I therefore concluded to leave many of them to time and events.

—Interview: July 12, 1891, *Douglass Papers*, ser. I, 5:461

Life

How to make the best of this life, as a thing of and for itself . . . must ever be an important and useful enquiry. For he who has best fitted himself to live and serve his fellow men on earth has best fitted himself to live and serve his God in Heaven, While in the world, a man's work is with the world and for the world. It is something to be a man among the shady trees and stately halls—but much more to be a man among men, full of the cares, labours, and joys of this life. It is good to think that in Heaven, all injustice, all wrong, all wars, all ignorance, and all vice, will be at an end; but how incomparably better is it, to wage a vigorous war upon these blighting evils and drive them from the present, so that the will of god may be done on earth as it is in heaven.

—Speech: "The Trials and Triumphs of Self-Made Men," January 4, 1860, *Douglass Papers*, ser. I, 3:290–91

Luck

Fortune may crowd a man's life with favorable circumstances and happy opportunities, but they will avail him nothing unless he makes a wise and vigorous use of them. It does not matter that the wind is fair and the tide at its flood, if the mariner refuses to weigh his anchor and spread his canvas to the breeze. The golden harvest is ripe in vain if the farmer refuses to reap. Opportunity is important but exertion is indispensable. "There is a tide in the affairs of men which, taken at its flood, leads on to fortune;" but it must be taken at its flood.

—Speech: "Self-Made Men," March 1893, *Douglass Papers*, ser. I, 5:553

Lynching

We are used to the shedding of innocent blood, and the heart of this nation is torpid, if not dead, to the national claims of justice and humanity, where the victims are of the colored race.

—Speech: "Strong to Suffer, and Yet Strong to Strive," April 16, 1886, *Douglass Papers*, ser. I, 5:228

The business of this nation is to protect its citizens *where they are*, not to transport them where they will not need protection.

—Autobiography: *Life and Times*, 1881, p. 341

Morality

The lesson taught by the history of nations is that the preservation or destruction of communities does not depend upon external prosperity. Men do not live by bread alone, so with nations, They are not saved by art, but by honesty. Not by the gilded splendors of wealth, but by the hidden treasure of manly virtue. Not by the multitudinous gratification of the flesh, but by the celestial guidance of the spirit.

    —Speech: "The Significance of Emancipation in the West Indies," August 3, 1857, *Douglass Papers*, ser. I, 3:193–94

Enforced morality is artificial morality.

    —Speech: "Who and What Is Woman?" May 24, 1886, *Douglass Papers*, ser. I, 5:258

Mothers

Never having enjoyed, to any considerable extent, her soothing presence, her tender and watchful care, I received the tidings of [my mother's] death with much the same emotions I should have probably felt at the death of a stranger.

    —Autobiography: *Narrative*, 1845, p. 14

I do not recollect ever seeing my mother by the light of day. She was with me in the night. She would lie down with me, and get me to sleep, but long before I waked she was gone.

    —Autobiography: *Narrative*, 1845, p. 14

My poor mother, like many other slave-women, had many children, but NO FAMILY!

    —Autobiography: *My Bondage and My Freedom*, 1855, p. 29

The practice of separating mothers from their children and hiring them out at distances too great to admit of their meeting, save at long intervals, was a marked feature of the cruelty and barbarity of the slave system; but it was in harmony with the grand aim of that system, which always and everywhere sought to reduce man to a level with the brute.

—Autobiography: *Life and Times,* 1881, p. 24

I was grander upon my mother's knee than a king upon his throne.

—Autobiography: *Life and Times,* 1881, p. 29

Young mothers who worked in the field were allowed an hour about ten o'clock in the morning to go home to nurse their children. This was when they were not required to take them to the field with them, and leave them upon "turning row," or in the corner of the fences.

—Autobiography: *Life and Times,* 1881, p. 46

Murder
(see also Capital Punishment)

A simple leaden bullet, and a few grains of powder, in the shortest limit of time, are sufficient to blast and ruin all that is precious in human existence, not alone of the murdered, but of the murderer.

—Autobiography: *Life and Times,* 1881, p. 291

It is not easy to reconcile human feeling to the shedding of blood for any purpose, unless indeed in the excitement which the shedding of blood itself occasions. The knife is to feeling always an offence, even when in the hands of a skilled surgeon; it refuses consent to the operation long after reason has demonstrated its necessity. It even pleads the cause of the known murderer on the day of his execution, and calls society half criminal when, in cold blood, it takes life as a protection of itself from crime. Let no word be said against this holy feeling; more than to law and government are we indebted to this tender sentiment of regard for human life for the safety with which we walk the streets by day and sleep secure in our beds at night. It is nature's grand police, vigilant and faithful, sentineled in the soul, guarding against violence to peace and life.

—Speech: "Did John Brown Fail?" May 30, 1881, *Douglass Papers*, ser. I, 5:10

Native Americans

(see also Assimilation)

The Indians, that noble race that once possessed this land, are fast passing from existence; they look upon their home, now the home of the white man; they look, with saddened eye, upon the graves of their fathers, profaned by the careless tread of the stranger; and they see that there is a power working their destruction, and they retreat before it.

—Speech: "Men and Brothers," May 7, 1850, *Douglass Papers*, ser. I, 2:242

The slaveholders have never kept a treaty when it was [in] their interests to break it. The history of the poor Indians in this country has yet to be written—the history of the southern tribes has yet to be told, and a tale of woe, of blood, of tears, and of perfidy will then be told of the southern States, sufficient to make men black as pandemonium itself. They have broken faith with every Indian tribe.

—Speech: "Bound Together in a Grand League of Freedom," June 21, 1854, *Douglass Papers*, ser. I, 2:497

The Indian, to be sure, is a stout man; he is proud and dignified; he is too stiff to bend, and breaks. he sees the plowshare of civilization casting up the bones of his venerated fathers, and he retires from the lakes to the mountains, and whenever he hears the hum of the honey bee he takes it for a warning to depart still farther from civilization. You see him going about with blankets upon him. He will not even imitate your wearing apparel, but clings to his blanket, lives in hollow trees, and, finally, dies.

—Speech: "Black Freedom Is the Prerequisite of Victory," January 13, 1865, *Douglass Papers*, ser. I, 4:57

There is a romantic reverence—a sort of hero-worship—paid the Indian all over this country; while the negro is despised; yet the Indiana rejects your civilization, and the negro accepts it. He is with you, of you, been here for the last two hundred and fifty years, braving the same latitudes, longitudes and altitudes in facing the same climate; enduring hardships that well might exterminate another people, yet living, flourishing with you, accepting all that is valuable in your civilization and serving you at every turn.

—Speech: "We Are Here and Want the Ballot Box," September 4, 1866, *Douglass Papers*, ser. I, 4:130

You see the Indian . . . refusing to imitate, refusing to follow the fashion . . . and the consequence is, that he dies or retreats before the onward march of your civilization—[whereas the black man] becomes just what other people become, and herein is the security for his continued life.

—Speech: "Let the Negro Alone," May 11, 1869, *Douglass Papers,* ser. I, 4:207–8

Nature

The day as fine, the heavens clear, the sun bright, the air salubrious, and the scenery by which we were surrounded extremely grand; all nature seemed redolent with anti-slavery truth.

—Correspondence: Douglass to James Miller McKim, September 5, 1844, *Douglass Papers,* ser. 3, 1:29

When a man confronts Niagara, for the first time in his life, he is awed into silence by the grandeur and sublimity of the scene. The voice of nature, so august and impressive, overwhelms the voice of art.

—Speech: "A Friendly Word to Maryland," November 17, 1864, *Douglass Papers,* ser. I, 4:41

Necessity

Necessity is not only the mother of invention, but the mainspring of exertion. The presence of some urgent, pinching, impervious necessity, will often not only sting a man into marvelous exertion, but into a sense of the possession, within himself, of powers and resources which else had slumbered on through a long life, unknown to himself and never suspected by others. A man never knows the strength of his grip till life and limb depend upon it. Something is likely to be done when something must be done.

—Speech: "Self-Made Men," March 1893, *Douglass Papers,* ser. I, 5:558

Nostalgia

I felt I had reached the end of the noblest and best part of my life; my school was broken up, my church disbanded, and the beloved congregation dispersed, never to come together again.
—Autobiography: *Life and Times,* 1881, p. 292

A man in the situation I found myself, has not only to divest himself of the old, which is never easily done, but to adjust himself to the new, which is still more difficult.
—Autobiography: *Life and Times,* 1881, p. 292

Whatever of good or ill the future may have in store for me, the past at least is secure.
—Autobiography: *Life and Times,* 1881, p. 318

My joys have far exceeded my sorrows and my friends have brought me far more than my enemies have taken from me.
—Autobiography: *Life and Times,* 1881, p. 372

Human nature itself has a warm and friendly side for what is old; for what has withstood the tide of time and become venerable with age.
—Speech: "It Moves," November 20, 1883, *Douglass Papers,* ser. I, 5:135

Oppression

This struggle may be a moral one, or it may be a physical one, and it may be both moral and physical, but is must be a struggle. Power concedes nothing without a demand. It never did and it never will. Find out just what any people will quietly submit to and you have found out the exact measure of injustice and wrong which will be imposed on them, and these will continue till they are resisted with either words or blows, or with both. The limits of tyrants are prescribed by the endurance of those whom they oppress. . . . Men may not get all they pay for in this world, but they must certainly pay for all they get. If we ever get free from the oppressions and wrongs heaped upon us, we must pay for their removal. We must do this by labor, by suffering, by sacrifice, and if needs be, by our lives and the lives of others.

—Speech: "The Significance of Emancipation in the West Indies," August 3, 1857, *Douglass Papers*, ser. I, 3:204

Oppression is apt to make even a wise man mad.

—Speech: "Eulogy of William Jay," May 12, 1859, *Douglass Papers*, ser. I, 3:257

Optimism

One of the most valuable lessons left us by this struggle of slavery is faith in man, faith in the rectitude of humanity, and faith in the all conquering power of truth as opposed to error—opposed to falsehood.

—Speech: "Recollections of the Anti-Slavery Conflict," April 21, 1873, *Douglass Papers*, ser. I, 4:367

Oratory

It was impossible for me to repeat the same old story month after month, and to keep up my interest in it. It was new to the people, it is true, but it was an old story to me; and to go through with it night after night, was a task altogether too mechanical for my nature.

—Autobiography: *My Bondage and My Freedom*, 1855, pp. 207–8

I have found that subjects, remote from public thought and feeling, are apt to prove even if not somewhat remote from the thought and feeling of the speaker himself, and that anything so remote cannot easily be made very interesting to any body.

—Speech: "Our National Capital," May 8, 1877, *Douglass Papers*, ser. I, 4:444

I found that the success of a lecturer depends more upon the quality of his stock in store than the amount.

—Autobiography: *Life and Times*, 1881, p. 294

I could never be brief, I never made a short speech in my life with which I was satisfied, nor a long speech with which anybody else was entirely satisfied.

—Speech: "Freedom Has Brought Duties," January 1, 1883, *Douglass Papers*, ser. I, 5:54

Great is the miracle of human speech—by it nations are enlightened and reformed; by it the cause of justice and liberty is defended, by it evils are exposed, ignorance dispelled, the path of duty made plain, and by it those that live to-day are put into the possession of the wisdom of ages gone by.

—Speech: "Great Is the Miracle of Human Speech," August 31, 1891, *Douglass Papers*, ser. I, 5:476–77

When a black man's language is quoted, in order to belittle and degrade him, his ideas are put into the most grotesque and unreadable

English, while the utterances of negro scholars and authors are ignored. A hundred white men will attend a concert of white negro minstrels with faces blackened with burnt cork, to one who will attend a lecture by an intelligent negro.

—Speech: "Lessons of the Hour," January 9, 1894, *Douglass Papers,* ser. I, 5:592

Parenting

If you wish to make your son helpless, you need not cripple him with bullet or bludgeon, but simply place him beyond the reach of necessity and surround him with ease and luxury. This experiment has often been tried and has seldom failed.

—Speech: "Self-Made Men," March 1893, *Douglass Papers,* ser. I, 5:558

Patriotism
(see also Declaration of Independence, Fourth of July)

I have no protection at home, or resting-place abroad. The land of my birth welcomes me to her shores only as a slave, and spurns with contempt the idea of treating me differently. So that I am an outcast from the society of my childhood, and an outlaw in the land of my birth. "I am a stranger with thee, and a sojourner as all my fathers were." That men should be patriotic is to me perfectly natural; and as a philosophical fact, I am able to give it an intellectual recognition. But no further can I go. If ever I had any patriotism, or any capacity for the feeling, it was whipt out of me long since by the lash of the American soul-drivers.

—Correspondence: Douglass to William Lloyd Garrison, January I, 1846, *Douglass Papers,* ser. 3, 1:73

In thinking of America, I sometimes find myself admiring her bright blue sky—her grand old woods—her fertile fields—her beautiful rivers—her mighty lakes, and star-crowned mountains. But my rapture is soon cursed with the infernal spirit of slaveholding, robbery and wrong,—when I remember that with the waters of her noblest rivers, the tears of my brethren are borne to the ocean, disregarded and forgotten, and that her most fertile fields drink daily of the warm blood of my outraged sisters, I am filled with unutterable loathing, and led to reproach myself that anything could fall from my lips in praise of such a land. America will not allow her children to love her. She seems bent on compelling those who would be her warmest friends, to be her worst enemies. May God give her repentance before it is too late, is the ardent prayer of my heart. I will continue to pray, labor, and wait, believing that she cannot always be insensible to the dictates of justice, or deaf to the voice of humanity.

—Correspondence: Douglass to William Lloyd Garrison, January 1, 1846, *Douglass Papers*, ser. 3, 1:73

I think I may boldly tell you that I am a republican, but not an American republican. I am here as a reviler of American republicanism. Aside from slavery I regard America as a brilliant example to the world; only wash from her escutcheon the bloody stain of slavery, and she will stand forth as a noble example for others to follow. But as long as the tears of my sisters and brother continue to run down her streams unheeded into the vast ocean of human misery, my tongue shall cleave to the roof of my mouth ere I speak as well of such a nation.

—Speech: "America's Compromise with Slavery and the Abolitionists' Work," April 6, 1846, *Douglass Papers*, ser. 1, 1:212

No, I make no pretension to patriotism. So long as my voice can be heard on this or the other side of the Atlantic, I shall hold up America to the lightning scorn of moral indignation. In doing this, I shall feel myself discharging the duty of a true patriot; for he is a lover of his country who rebukes and does not excuse its sins. It is righteousness that exalteth a nation while sin is a reproach to any people.

—Speech: "Love of God, Love of Man, Love of Country," September 24, 1847, *Douglass Papers*, ser. I, 2:103

He who will, intelligently, lay down his life for his country, is a man whom it is not in human nature to despise. Your fathers staked their lives, their fortunes, and their sacred honor, on the cause of their country. In their admiration of liberty, they lost sight of all other interests.

—Speech: "What to the Slave Is the Fourth of July?" July 5, 1852, *Douglass Papers*, ser. I, 2:364

What, to the American slave, is your 4th of July? I answer: a day that reveals to him, more than all other days of the year, the gross injustice and cruelty to which he is the constant victim. To him, your celebration is a sham. . . .

—Speech: "What to the Slave Is the Fourth of July?" July 5, 1852, *Douglass Papers*, ser. I, 2:371

He who will, intelligently, lay down his life for his country, is a man whom it is not in human nature to despise.

—Speech: "What to the Slave Is the Fourth of July?" July 5, 1852, *Douglass Papers*, ser. I, 2:364

The man who limits his admiration of good actions to the country in which he happens to be born, (if he ever was born,) or to the nation or community of which he forms a small part, is a most pitiable object. With him to be one of a nation is more than to be one of the human family. He don't live in the world, but he lives in the United States.

Into his little soul the thought of God as our common Father, and of man our common Brother has never entered.

—Speech: "The Significance of Emancipation in the West Indies," August 3, 1857, *Douglass Papers*, ser. I, 3:199

Peace

The people in this country who take the deepest interest in the removal of Slavery from America and the spread of Liberty throughout the world, are the same who oppose the bloody spirit of war, and are earnestly laboring to spread the blessings of peace all over the globe.

—Correspondence: Douglass to Horace Greeley, April 15, 1846, *Douglass Papers*, ser. 3, 1:105

He was a peace man—but his peace principles only led him to be peaceable towards those to whom peace was a blessing, and was really appropriate. He was not for "casting pearls before swine." He was for the peace of which God himself was in favour—peace for well-doing; but he was not for a peace where there was oppression, injustice, or outrage upon the right,—none but the most hollow and deceitful peace could ever exist between the man who was on his back on the ground, and the man who stood on his neck with his heel. The Divine argument was this, be first "pure and then peaceable."

—Speech: "John Brown and the Slaveholders' Insurrection," January 30, 1860, *Douglass Papers*, ser. I, 3:317

Peace between races is not to be secured by degrading one race and exalting another, by giving power to one race and withholding it from another, but by maintaining a state of equal justice between all classes.

—Autobiography: *Life and Times*, 1881, p. 301

People

The American people may be accurately measured by the character of her great men, as the degree of temperature may be determined by the face of the thermometer,

—Speech: "Of Morals and Men," May 8, 1849, *Douglass Papers*, ser. I, 2:172

John Brown

To the outward eye, John Brown was a criminal, but to their inward eye he was a just man and true. His deeds might be disowned, but the spirit which made those deeds possible was worthy highest honor.

—Speech: "Did John Brown Fail?" May 30, 1881, *Douglass Papers*, ser. I, 5:21

With the Allegheny mountains for his pulpit, the country for his church and the whole civilized world for his audience, he was a thousand times more effective as a preacher than as a warrior, and the consciousness of this fact was the secret of his amazing complacency. Mighty with the sword of steel, he was mightier with the sword of truth, and with this sword he literally swept the horizon. He was more than a match for all the Wises, Masons, Vallandighams and Washingtons, who could rise against him. They could kill him, but they could not answer him.

—Speech: "Did John Brown Fail?" May 30, 1881, *Douglass Papers*, ser. I, 5:23

If John Brown did not end the war that ended slavery, he did at least begin the war that ended slavery. If we look over the dates, places and men for which this honor is claimed, we shall find that not Carolina, not Virginia, not Fort Sumter, but Harpers Ferry, and the United

States Arsenal, not Major Anderson, but John Brown began the war that ended slavery and made this a free republic. Until this blow was struck, the prospect for Freedom was dim, shadowy and uncertain. The irrepressible conflict was one with words, votes and compromises. When John Brown stretched forth his arm the sky was cleared—the time for compromise was gone—the armed hosts stood face to face over a chasm of a broken Union and the clash of arms was at hand.

—Speech: "Did John Brown Fail?" May 30, 1881, *Douglass Papers,* ser. I, 5:35

His body was in the dust, but his soul was marching on. His defeat was already assuming the form and pressure of victory, and his death was giving new life and power to the principles of justice and liberty.

—Autobiography: *Life and Times,* 1881, p. 253

John C. Calhoun

The very spirit of Mr. Calhoun animates the slavery party of to-day. His principles are its principles, and his philosophy, its philosophy. He looked upon slavery as the great American interest. The slavery of to-day so esteem it.

—Speech: "Slavery, Freedom, and the Kansas-Nebraska Act," October 30, 1854, *Douglass Papers,* ser. I, 2:546

Grover Cleveland

[T]here was nothing in the bearing of Mr. and Mrs. Cleveland toward Mrs. Douglass and myself less cordial and courteous than that extended to the other ladies and gentlemen present. This manly defiance, by a Democratic President, of a malignant and time-honored prejudice, won my respect for the courage of Mr. Cleveland.

—Autobiography: *Life and Times,* 1881, p. 392

Christopher Columbus

Christopher Columbus, the man who saw by an eye of faith the things hoped for and the evidence of things not seen. . . .

—Autobiography: *Life and Times,* 1881, p. 418

James A. Garfield

His amiable disposition to make himself agreeable to those with whom he came in contact made him weak and led him to create false hopes in those who approached him for favors.

—Autobiography: *Life and Times,* 1881, p. 385

William Lloyd Garrison

Of my friend Mr. Garrison, and I call him my friend in no platform sense of the term; I feel him to be my friend—the friend of the friendless—the friend of the slave—the friend of the negro in the United States. . . .

—Speech: "A Call for the British Nation to Testify against Slavery," August 28, 1846, *Douglass Papers,* ser. I, 1:362

Seventeen years ago, few men possessed a more heavenly countenance than William Lloyd Garrison, and few men evinced a more genuine or a more exalted piety. The bible was his text book—held sacred, as the word of the Eternal father—sinless perfection—complete submission to insults and injuries—literal obedience to the injunction, if smitten on one side to turn the other also. Not only was Sunday a Sabbath, but all days a week sabbaths, and to be kept holy. All sectarianism false and mischievous—the regenerated, throughout the world, members of one body, and the HEAD Christ Jesus. Prejudice against color was rebellion against God. Of all men beneath the sky, the slaves, because most neglected and despised, were nearest and dearest to his great heart.

—Autobiography: *My Bondage and My Freedom,* 1855, p. 204

No wonder that in their moral blindness men called him a fanatic and a madman, for against such odds it was thought that nothing but madness would venture to contend. But there was nothing of madness in the composition of William Lloyd Garrison, or in his espousal of the cause to which he gave his mind and heart.

—Speech: "This Is a Sad and Mournful Hour," June 2, 1879, *Douglass Papers*, ser. I, 4:505

He was a grand man, a moral hero, a man whose acquaintance and friendship it was a great privilege to enjoy. While liberty has a friend on earth, and slavery an earnest enemy, his name and his works will be held in profound and grateful memory.

—Speech: "Our Destiny Is Largely in Our Own Hands," April 16, 1883, *Douglass Papers*, ser. I, 5:68

Ulysses S. Grant

My confidence in Gen. [Ulysses S.] Grant was not entirely due to the brilliant military successes achieved by him, but there was a moral as well as military basis for my faith in him. He has shown his single mindedness and superiority to popular prejudice by his prompt co-operation with President Lincoln in his policy of employing colored troops, and his order commanding his soldiers to treat such troops with due respect.

—Autobiography: *Life and Times*, 1881, p. 279

[A]fter Lincoln and Sumner no man in his intercourse with me gave evidence of more freedom from vulgar prejudice. . . .

—Editorial, "U.S. Grant and the Colored People," *New National Era*, n.d., in Benjamin Quarles, *Frederick Douglass* [1948] (New York: Da Capo Press, 1997), p. 262

Andrew Johnson

No stronger contrast could well be presented between two men than between President Lincoln and Vice-President Johnson on this day. Mr. Lincoln was like one who was treading the hard and thorny path of duty and self-denial; Mr. Johnson was like one just from a drunken debauch. The face of the one was full of manly humility, although at the topmost height of power and pride, the other was full of pomp and swaggering vanity. The fact was, though it was yet early in the day, Mr. Johnson was drunk.

—Autobiography: *Life and Times*, 1881, p. 285

Abraham Lincoln

He is a man of the people. He came up from among them, and that by the native energy of his character and his manly industry. I am ever pleased to see a man rise from among the people. Every such man is prophetic of the good time coming.

—Speech: "Slavery, Freedom, and the Kansas-Nebraska Act," October 30, 1854, *Douglass Papers*, ser. I, 2:541

I came to the conclusion that while Abraham Lincoln will not go down to posterity as Abraham the Great, or as Abraham the Wise, or as Abraham the Eloquent, although he is all three, wise, great, and eloquent, he will go down to posterity, if the country is saved, as Honest Abraham; and going down thus, his name may be written anywhere in this wide world of ours side by side with that of Washington, without disparaging the latter.

—Speech: "Emancipation, Racism, and the Work before Us," December 4, 1863, *Douglass Papers*, ser. 3, 3:608

To-day [The Death of Lincoln], to-day as never before this North is a unit! To-day, to-day as never before, the American people, although they know they cannot have indemnity for the past—for the countless treasure and the precious blood—yet they resolve to-day that they will enact ample security for the future! And if it teaches us this lesson, it may be that the blood of our beloved martyred President will be the salvation of our country. Good man we call him, good man he was. If "an honest man is the noblest work of God," we need have no fear for the soul of Abraham Lincoln.

—Speech: "Our Martyred President," April 15, 1865, *Douglass Papers*, ser. I, 4:78

He was a self-made man, a rail-splitter, the captain of a flatboat; he took hold of life in the rough of it. He travelled far, but he made the road in which he advanced; he climbed high, but he made the ladder on which he ascended. This will ever make the name of Abraham Lincoln dear to all the toilers of our land.

—Speech: "The Assassination and Its Lessons," February 13, 1866, *Douglass Papers*, ser. I, 4:110

He was preeminently the white man's President, entirely devoted to the welfare of white men. He was ready and willing at any time during the last years of his administration to deny, postpone and sacrifice the rights of humanity in the colored people, to promote the welfare of the white people of his country.

—Speech: "The Freedmen's Monument to Abraham Lincoln," April 14, 1876, *Douglass Papers*, ser. I, 4:431

YOU ARE THE CHILDREN of Abraham Lincoln. We are at best only his step-children, children by adoption, children by force of circumstances and necessity. To you it especially belongs to sound his praises, to preserve and perpetuate his memory, to multiply his statues, to hang his pictures on your walls, and commend his example, for to you he was a great and glorious friend and benefactor.

—Speech: "The Freedmen's Monument to Abraham Lincoln," April 14, 1876, *Douglass Papers*, ser. I, 4:432

Any man can say things that are true of Abraham Lincoln. His personal traits and public acts are better known to the American people than are those of any other man of his age. He was a mystery to no man who saw him and heard him. Though high in position, the humblest could approach him and feel at home in his presence. Though deep, he was transparent; though strong, he was gentle; though decided and pronounced in his convictions, he was tolerant towards those who differed from him, and patient under reproaches.

—Speech: "The Freedmen's Monument to Abraham Lincoln," April 14, 1876, *Douglass Papers*, ser. I, 4:436

Viewed from the genuine abolition ground, Mr. Lincoln seemed tardy, cold, dull, and indifferent; but measuring him by the sentiment of his country, a sentiment he was bound as a statesman to consult, he was swift, zealous, radical, and determined.

—Speech: "The Freedmen's Monument to Abraham Lincoln," April 14, 1876, *Douglass Papers*, ser. I, 4:436

I was never more quickly or more completely put at ease in the presence of a great man than in that of Abraham Lincoln.

—Autobiography: *Life and Times*, 1881, p. 271

Mr. Lincoln was not only a great President, but a GREAT MAN— too great to be small in anything. In his company I was never in any way reminded of my humble origin, or of my unpopular color.

—Autobiography: *Life and Times*, 1881, p. 281

The South was not far behind the North in recognizing Abraham Lincoln as the natural leader of the rising political sentiment of the country against slavery, and it was equally quick in its efforts to counteract and destroy his influence. Its papers teemed with the bitterest invectives against the "back-woodsman of Illinois," the "flat-boatman," the "rail-splitter," the "third-rate lawyer," and much else and worse.

—Autobiography: *Life and Times,* 1881, p. 230

He alone of all our Presidents was to have the opportunity to destroy slavery, and to lift into manhood millions of his countrymen hitherto held as chattels and numbered with the beasts of the field.

—Autobiography: *Life and Times,* 1881, p. 254

After the fall of Richmond the collapse of the rebellion was not long delayed, though it did not perish without adding to its long list of atrocities one which sent a thrill of horror throughout the civilized world, in the assassination of Abraham Lincoln; a man so amiable, so kind, humane, and honest, that one is at a loss to know how he could have had an enemy on earth.

—Autobiography: *Life and Times,* 1881, pp. 289–90

Men called him homely, and homely he was; but it was manifestly a human homeliness, for there was nothing of the tiger or other wild animal about him. His eyes had in them the tenderness of motherhood, and his mouth and other features the highest perfection of genuine manhood.

—Autobiography: *Life and Times,* 1881, pp. 290–91

Lucretia Mott

Great as this woman was in speech, and persuasive as she was in her writings, she was incomparably greater in her presence. She spoke to the world through every line of her countenance. In her there was no lack of symmetry—no contradiction between her thought and act. Seated in an anti-slavery meeting, looking benignantly around upon the assembly, her silent presence made others eloquent, and carried the argument home to the heart of the audience.

—Autobiography: *Life and Times*, 1881, p. 367

The known approval of such a woman of any cause, went far to commend it.

—Autobiography: *Life and Times*, 1881, p. 367

Wendell Phillips

It is true that Mr. Phillips was a friend to temperance, to the cause of the working-classes, and to Ireland. Wherever the tyrant reared his head, he was ready, like O'Connell, to deal his bolts upon it. But he was primarily and pre-eminently the colored man's friend, not because the colored man was colored, not because he was of a different variety of the human family from himself, but because he was a man, and fully entitled to enjoy all the rights and immunities of manhood. The cause of the slave was his first love; and from it he never wavered, but was true and steadfast through life.

—Speech: "Wendell Phillips Cast His Lot with the Slave," *Douglass Papers*, ser. I, 5:151–52

Harriet Beecher Stowe

Happy woman must she be that to her was given the power in such unstinted measure to touch and move the popular heart! More than to reason or religion are we indebted to the influence which this wonderful delineation of American chattel slavery produced on the public mind.

—Autobiography: *Life and Times*, 1881, p. 369

Photography

Byron says, a man always looks *dead*, when his Biography is written. The same is even more true when his picture is taken. There is ever something statue-like about such men. See them when or where you will, and unless they are totally off guard, they are either serenely sitting, or rigidly standing in what they fancy their best attitude for a picture.

—Speech: "Pictures and Progress," December 3, 1861, *Douglass Papers*, ser. I, 3:455

Success is the admitted standard of American greatness and it is marvelous to observe how readily it also becomes the [ideal] standard of manly beauty. There is a marked improvement in the features of the successful man, and a corresponding deterioration in those of the unsuccessful. Our military heroes look better even in pictures, after winning an important battle, than after losing one. The pictures do not change, but we look at them through the favorable or unfavorable prevailing public opinion.

—Speech: "Pictures and Progress," December 3, 1861, *Douglass Papers*, ser. I, 3:457

Next to bad manuscripts, pictures can be made the greatest bores. Authors, Editors, and printers suffer by the former, while almost every body has suffered by the latter. They are pushed at you in every house you enter, and what is worse you are required to give an opinion of them.

—Speech: "Pictures and Progress," December 3, 1861, *Douglass Papers*, ser. I, 3:458

Politics

(see also Government)

Agitation

Endure unto the end, there is about Truth an inherent vitality, a recuperative energy. . . . Progression is the law of our being.

—Editorial: "The Suffrage Question," *Frederick Douglass' Paper,*
April 25, 1856

No genuine tyrant surrenders his scepter without a struggle.

—Speech: We Are Not Yet Quite Free," August 3, 1869, *Douglass Papers,* ser. I, 4:221

If there is no struggle there is no progress. Those who profess to favor freedom and yet deprecate agitation, are men who want crops without plowing up the ground, they want rain without thunder and lightning. They want the ocean without the awful roar of its many waters. This struggle may be a moral one, or it may be a physical one, and it may be both moral and physical, but it must be a struggle. Power concedes nothing without a demand. It never did and it never will.

—Speech: "The Significance of Emancipation in the West Indies,"
August 3, 1857, *Douglass Papers,* ser. I, 3:204

You know that liberty given is never so precious as liberty sought for and fought for. The man outraged is the man to make the outcry. Depend upon it, men will not care much for a people who do not care for themselves.

—Speech: "Parties Were Made for Men, Not Men for Parties,"
September 25, 1883, Douglass Papers, ser. I, 5:95

Compromise

The anti-slavery cause has, from the beginning, suffered more from the compromising and temporizing spirit of the politicians who have undertaken to serve it, than from the assaults of its open and undisguised enemies. It has often been more injured by the *"ifs"* and "buts" of politicians, than by the brickbats and unsalable eggs of the proslavery mob.

—Speech: "The American Apocalypse," June 16, 1861, *Douglass Papers,* ser. 3, 3:440–47

There is a middle path—We have pursued that middle path. It is compromise and by it we have reached the point of civil war with all its horrid consequences. The question is shall we start anew in the same old path?

—Speech: "The War and How to End It," March 25, 1862, *Douglass Papers,* ser. 1, 3:520

Conventions

Because conventions of the people are in themselves harmless and when made the means of setting forth grievances, whether real or fancied, they are the safety-valves of the Republic, a wise and safe substitute for violence, dynamite and all sorts of revolutionary action against peace and good order of society.

—Speech: "Parties Were Made for Men, Not Men for Parties," September 25, 1883, *Douglass Papers,* ser. 1, 5:90

Democratic Party

I have a great respect for a certain quality for which the Democratic party is distinguished. That quality is fidelity to its friends, its faithfulness to those whom it has acknowledged as its masters during the last forty years. It was faithful to the slave holding class during the existence of slavery. It was faithful to them before the war. It gave them all the encouragement that it possibly could without drawing its own neck into the halter. It was also faithful during the period of reconstruction and it has been faithful ever since.

—Autobiography: *Life and Times,* 1881, p. 437

Independents

No man can serve two masters in politics any more than in religion. If there is one position in life more despicable in the eyes of man, and more condemned by nature than another, it is that of neutrality. Besides, if there is one thing more impossible than another, it is a position of perfect neutrality in politics.

—Speech: "Strong to Suffer, and Yet Strong to Strive," April 16, 1886, *Douglass Papers,* ser. I, 5:234

Moderates

They stand between the two extremes; men who compliment themselves for their moderation, because they are neither hot nor cold; men who sometimes help a good cause a little in order to hinder it a great deal. They are, however, of little account in the conflict with evil. They are mere drift wood; what sailors call dead water. They follow in the wake of their respective forces, being themselves destitute of motive power.

—Speech: "It Moves," November 20, 1883, *Douglass Papers,* ser. I, 5:144

Partisanship

[P]olitical parties, like individual men, are only strong while they are consistent and honest, and that treachery and deception are only the sand on which political fools vainly endeavor to build.

—Autobiography: *Life and Times,* 1881, p. 394

[T]he Republican party was the party hated by the old master class, and that the Democratic party was the party beloved of the old master class.
—Autobiography: *Life and Times,* 1881, p. 395

I have always felt that in the presence of the oppression and persecution to which the colored race is subjected in the Southern States, no colored man can consistently base his support of any party upon any other principle than that which looks to the protection of men and women from lynch law and murder.
—Autobiography: *Life and Times,* 1881, p. 439

One great lesson taught by Republican defeat is familiar to all. It is the folly of relying upon past good behavior for present success. Parties, like men, must act in the living present or fail. It is not what they have done or left undone in the past that turns the scale, but what they are doing, and mean to do now. The result shows that neither the past good conduct of the Republican party nor the past bad conduct of the Democratic party has had much to do with the late election.
—Speech: "We Are Confronted by a New Administration," April 16, 885, *Douglass Papers,* ser. I, 5:178

Though I am a party man, to me parties are valuable only as they subserve the ends of good government. When they persistently violate the fundamental rights of the humblest and weakest in the land I scout them, despise them, and leave them.
—Speech: "We Are Confronted by a New Administration," April 16, 1885, *Douglass Papers,* ser. I, 5:184–85

Republican Party

You are called Black Republicans. What right have you to that name? Among all the Candidates you have selected, or talked of, I have not seen or heard of a single black one. Nor have I seen one mentioned with any prospect of success, who is friendly to the black man in his sympathies, or an advocate for the restoration of his rights.

—Speech: "The Political Response to Slavery's Aggressions," May 28, 1856, *Douglass Papers,* ser. I, 3:141

Gentleman, I am a republican, a radial republican, a Black republican, a republican dyed in the wool, and for one I want the republican party to live as long as I do. Few greater calamities could befall the country, in my judgment, at any time within the next dozen years, than the defeat and disbandment of the Republican party. To its courage in war, and to its wisdom in peace, we are indebted for whatever light that now illumes our national future. It is the party of law and order, of liberty and of progress, of honor and honesty, as against disloyalty, moral stagnation, dishonest voting, and repudiation. While that party is in power nobody doubts that the national integrity will be maintained, that personal liberty will be secure, that the national progress will be steady, that the national debt will be duly acknowledged and paid, and that our country will be a country of peace and prosperity.

—Speech: "I Speak to You as an American Citizen," October I, 1870, *Douglass Papers,* ser. I, 4:275

For the colored men the Republican party is the deck, all outside is the sea.

—Speech: "The Republican Party Must Be Maintained in Power," April 13, 1872, *Douglass Papers,* ser. I, 4:298

Tyranny
How the monarchs and aristocrats of the old world will tremble at the rapid march of republican freedom! How they will hide their eyes for very shame, when they think of their own tyranny, in comparison with

the free and noble institutions of America,—where freedom of the press means freedom to advocate slavery, and where liberty regulated by law means slavery protected by an armed band of bloody assassins! But, thank Heaven! "Oppression shall not always reign."

—Correspondence: Douglass to William Lloyd Garrison, September 16, 1845, *Douglass Papers*, ser. 3, 1:53

Let us render the tyrant no aid; let us not hold the light by which he can trace the footprints of our flying brother.

—Autobiography: *Narrative*, 1845, p. 71

The only penetrable point of a tyrant is the *fear of death*. The outcry they make, as to the danger of having their throats cut is because they deserve to have them *cut*.

—Correspondence: Douglass to Editor of the Rochester *Democrat and American*, October 31, 1859, in Philip S. Foner, *The Life and Writings of Frederick Douglass*, 5 vols. (New York: International Publishers, 1950–75), 2:461

Poverty

Poverty is our greatest calamity. It draws down upon us the very condition which makes us a helpless, hopeless, dependent, and dispirited people, the target for the contempt and scorn of all around us.

—Speech: "Agriculture and Black Progress," September 18, 1873, *Douglass Papers*, ser. 1, 4:393

Weeds do not more naturally spring out of a manure pile than crime out of enforced destitution.

—Speech: "Parties Were Made for Men, Not Men for Parties," September 25, 1883, *Douglass Papers*, ser. 1, 5:101

The Press

In America, and I believe in this country [Scotland], it is understood as being but common fairness, when either a single individual or a body of individuals are attacked in their opinions or conduct in the columns of a newspaper, that he or they have an opportunity of reply through the same columns, so that the cup containing the poison, or supposed poison, may also contain its antidote. This in America is established etiquette; it is also common fairness and common justice. It is only where this etiquette is established in a community that it can be said to have any of the advantages of a public press, that it becomes the palladium of liberty as well as of purity. But let the opposite principle prevail, and it is a curse rather than a blessing. No man is safe! He may be pierced through with a thousand poisoned weapons, and be totally without the means of defense or redress.

—Speech: "Charges and Defense of the Free Church," March 10, 1846, *Douglass Papers*, ser. I, 1:173

A still greater misfortune to the negro is that the press, that engine of omnipotent power, usually tries him in advance of the courts, and when once his case is decided in the newspapers, it is easy for the jury to bring in its verdict of "guilty as indicted."

—Speech: "Our Destiny Is Largely in Our Own Hands," April 16, 1883, *Douglass Papers*, ser. I, 5:63–64

Principles

Nevertheless, I would not give up a just principle because it has been slower of adoption than a principle less just.

—Speech: "The Anti-Slavery Movement," March 18, 1855, *Douglass Papers*, ser. I, 3:23

Progress

We hear and read much of the achievements of this nineteenth century, and much can be said, and truthfully said of them. The world has literally shot forward with the speed of steam and lightning. It has probably made more progress during the last fifty years, than in any five hundred years to which we can refer in the history of the race. Knowledge has been greatly increased, and its blessing, widely diffused. Locomotion has been marvelously improved, so that the very ends of the earth are being rapidly brought together. Time of the traveler has been annihilated.

—Speech: "The Significance of Emancipation in the West Indies," August 3, 1857, *Douglass Papers*, ser. I, 3:191

All wishes, all aspirations, all hopes, all fears, all doubts, all determinations, grow stronger precisely in proportion as they get themselves expressed in words, forms[,] colours, and actions.

—Speech: "Pictures and Progress," December 3, 1861, *Douglass Papers*, ser. I, 3:461

The choice which life presents, is ever more, between growth and decay, perfection and deterioration. There is no standing still, nor can be. Advance or recede, occupy or give place—are the stern imperatives self existing and self enforcing law of life, from the cradle to the grave.

—Speech: "Pictures and Progress," December 3, 1861, *Douglass Papers*, ser. I, 3:471

Conceive of life without progress and sun[,] moon and stars instantly halt in their courses.

—Speech: "Pictures and Progress," December 3, 1861, *Douglass Papers*, ser. I, 3:471–22

Material progress, may for a time be separated from moral progress. But the two cannot be permanently divorced.

 —Speech: "Pictures and Progress," December 3, 1861, *Douglass Papers,* ser. I, 3:472

The world has never advanced a single inch in the right direction, when the movement could not be traced to some such small beginning.

 —Speech: "The Proclamation and a Negro Army," February 6, 1863, *Douglass Papers,* ser. 3, 3:564

When you talk about deprecating discussion, opposition, argument, are you blind to the fact that there is no backward flow of ideas, more than of rivers? . . . Stepping onward is glory.

 —Speech: "Govern with Magnanimity and Courage," September 6, 1866, *Douglass Papers,* ser. I, 4:140

[W]ithout property, there can be no leisure. Without leisure, there can be no thought. Without thought, there can be no invention. Without invention, there can be no progress.

 —Speech: "Agriculture and Black Progress," September 18, 1873, *Douglass Papers,* ser. I, 4:393

The progress of a nation is sometimes indicated by small things.

 —Autobiography: *Life and Times,* 1881, p. 327

The American people have their prejudices, [but] all their tendency is to progress, enlightenment and to the universal.

 —Speech: "Our Destiny Is Largely in Our Own Hands," April 16, 1883, *Douglass Papers,* ser. I, 5:80

A denial of progress and the assumption of retrogression is a point-blank contradiction to the ascertained and essential nature of man.

It opposes the known desire for change, and denies the instinctive hope and aspiration of humanity for something better.

—Speech: "It Moves," November 20, 1883, *Douglass Papers*, ser. I, 5:129

[T]he progress of society is in the direction of refinement and spirituality. Some form of grossness is eliminated with every step upward of the race. It is in accordance with the divine order. Not that which is spiritual is first, but that which is natural; after that, that which is spiritual.

—Speech: "Who and What Is Woman?" May 24, 1886, *Douglass Papers*, ser. I, 5:251

In tracing the moral and intellectual progress of mankind from barbarism to civilization, we see that any and every advance, however simple and reasonable, has been sternly resisted. It appears that the more simple the proposition of reform, the more stern and passionate has been the resistance. Victory has always been found, when found at all, on the other side of the battle field.

—Speech: "I Am a Radical Woman Suffrage Man," May 28, 1888, *Douglass Papers*, ser. I, 5:386

If we can't think we can't invent, if we can't invent we can make no discoveries, and if we make no discoveries there can be no progress.

—Speech: "Boyhood in Baltimore," September 6, 1891, *Douglass Papers*, ser. I, 5:484

Property
(see also Constitution, Slavery)

Assuming that the Constitution guaranteed their rights of property in their fellowmen, they held it to be in open violation of the Constitution for any American citizen in any part of the United States to speak, write, or act against this right.

—Autobiography: *Life and Times*, 1881, p. 217

[Contrary to what] we have so long heard in our pulpits so far from being a sin to accumulate property, it is the plain duty of every man to lay up something for the future. . . . I am for making the best of both worlds and making the best of this world first, because it comes first.

—Speech: "Great Britain's Example Is High, Noble, and Grand," August 6, 1885, *Douglass Papers*, ser. I, 5:208

Prosperity
(see also Freedman's Savings and Trust Bank)

Money he regarded as a great power. He who had money would not occupy a degraded position; hence he advised his young hearers to be economical to be rich, for the possession of wealth would tend greatly to advance them to that position, socially, to which they were entitled.

—Speech: "Advice to Black Youth," February 1, 1855, *Douglass Papers*, ser. I, 3:4

Public Opinion

If we wish to call attention to anything we may point at Britain. We learn what is the mind of Britain by reading the writings of such men as Dickens, as well as by the public press. I believe that the notice of Dickens had more effect in calling attention to the subject, than all the books published in America for ten years.

—Speech: "British Influence on the Abolition Movement in America," April 17, 1846, *Douglass Papers*, ser. I, 1:220

Public opinion is, indeed, an unfailing restraint upon the cruelty and barbarity of masters, overseers, and slave-drivers, whenever and wherever it can reach them; but there are certain secluded and out-of-the way places, even in the state of Maryland, seldom visited by a single ray of healthy public sentiment—where slavery, wrapt in its own congenial, midnight darkness, *can*, and *does*, develop all its malign and shocking characteristics; where it can be indecent without shame, cruel without shuddering, and murderous without apprehension or fear of exposure.

—Autobiography: *My Bondage and My Freedom*, 1855, p. 37

To be a restraint upon cruelty and vice, public opinion must emanate from a humane and virtuous community.

—Autobiography: *My Bondage and My Freedom*, 1855, p. 38

Such is the power of public opinion, that it is hard, even for the innocent, to feel the happy consolations of innocence, when they fall under the maledictions of this power. How could we regard ourselves as in the right, when all about us denounced us as criminals, and had the power and disposition to treat us as such.

—Autobiography: *My Bondage and My Freedom*, 1855, p. 170

Racism

Trampled, reviled and maltreated as I have been by white people During the most of my life—early taught to regard myself, their divinely appointed prey, and ever looking upon such as my natural enemies,—you may readily imagine the grateful emotions that thrill my heart when I meet with facts—forever dispelling the darkness of such infernal doctrines.

—Correspondence: Douglass to Richard Dowden, November 11, 1845, *Douglass Papers*, ser. 3, 1:66

You have no prejudices against blacks—no more than against any other color—but it is against the black man appearing as the colored gentleman. He is then a contradiction of your theory of natural inferiority in the colored race.

—Speech: "The Colonizationist Revival," May 31, 1849, *Douglass Papers*, ser. I, 2:210

[W]e are esteemed less than strangers and sojourners—aliens we are in our native land. . . . We are literally scourged beyond the beneficent range of both authorities, human and divine. . . . American humanity hates us, scorns us, disowns and denies our personality.

—Speech: "A Nation in the Midst of a Nation," May 11, 1853, *Douglass Papers*, ser. I, 2:425.

I deny that the black man's degradation is essential to the white man's elevation. I deny that, that the black man should be tied, lest he outstrip you in the race of improvement. I deny the existence of any such necessity, and affirm that those who allege the existence of any such, pay a sorry compliment to the white race.

—Speech: "A Friendly Word to Maryland," November 17, 1864, *Douglass Papers*, ser. I, 4:48

It is the misfortune of our class that it fails to derive due advantage from the achievements of its individual members, but never fails to suffer from the ignorance or crimes of a single individual with whom the class is identified.

—Speech: "The Douglass Institute," September 29, 1865, *Douglass Papers*, ser. I, 4:91

Wonderfully tenacious is the taint of a great moral wrong. The evil that men do lives after them. Slavery is dead, but its long, black shadow, in the form of prejudice, stretches broadly across our whole country, and will do so for some time yet to come. The American people are accustomed to seeing the black men at the back door, and are filled with doubts when they see him at the front door.

— Speech: "The Country Has Not Heard the Last of P. B. S. Pinchback," March 13, 1876, *Douglass Papers*, ser. I, 4:424

I know it is hard for a Turk to do justice to a Christian; hard for a Christian to do justice to a Jew; hard for an Englishman to do justice to an Irishman; hard for an Irishman to do justice to an Englishman;, and we all know that it is hard for a white man to do justice to a black man.

— Speech: "The Country Has Not Heard the Last of P. B. S. Pinchback," March 13, 1876, *Douglass Papers*, ser. I, 4:425

While a slave there was a mountain of gold on his breast to keep him down—now that he is free there is a mountain of prejudice to hold him down.

— Speech: "Our Destiny Is Largely in Our Own Hands," April 16, 1883, *Douglass Papers*, ser. I, 5:62

Take his relation to the national government and we shall find him a deserted, a defrauded, a swindled, and an outcast man. In law, free; in fact, a slave. In law, a citizen; in fact, an alien; in law, a voter; in fact, a disenfranchised man. In law his color is no crime; in fact, his color exposes him to be treated as a criminal. Toward him every attribute of a just government is contradicted.

— Speech: "In Law Free; in Fact, a Slave," April 16, 1888, *Douglass Papers*, ser. I, 5:369

When an unknown man is spoken of in their presence, the first question that arises in the average American mind concerning him and which must be answered is, Of what color is he? and he rises or falls in estimation by the answer given.

—Autobiography: *Life and Times,* 1881, p. 376

We want no aggrieved class in America. Strong as we are without the negro, we are stronger with him than without him. The power and friendship of seven millions of people, however humble and scattered all over the country are not to be despised.

—Autobiography: *Life and Times,* 1881, p. 401

Prejudice sets all logic at defiance. It takes no account of reason or consistency.

—Autobiography: *Life and Times,* 1881, p. 443

Interracial Marriage

If any such ban [of nature] existed, artificial "bans" such as legal enactments and popular prejudices would not be necessary to keep the races asunder. Nature would do her work.

—Correspondence: Douglass to Gerrit Smith, September 8, 1862, in Quarles, *Frederick Douglass,* p. 197

People who had remained silent over the unlawful relations of the white slave masters with their colored slave women loudly condemned me for marrying a wife a few shades lighter than myself. They would have no objection to my marrying a person much darker in complexion than myself, but to marry one much lighter and of the complexion of my father rather than of that of my mother, was, in the popular eye, a shocking offense, and one for which I was to be ostracized by white and black alike.

—Autobiography: *Life and Times,* 1881, p. 392

All this excitement . . . is caused by my marriage with a woman a few shades lighter than myself. If I had married a black woman there would have been nothing said about it. Yet the disparity in our complexions would have been the same.

—Interview: "God Almighty Made but One Race," January 25, 1884, *Douglass Papers*, ser. I, 5:146

I conceive . . . that there is no division of races, God Almighty made but one race. I adopt the theory that in time the varieties of races will be blended into one.

—Interview: "God Almighty Made but One Race," January 25, 1884, *Douglass Papers*, ser. I, 5:147

Origins

While we are servants, we are never offensive to the whites, or marks of popular displeasure. . . . The evil lies deeper than prejudice against color. It is, as we have said, an intense hatred of the colored man when he is distinguished for any ennobling qualities of head or heart.

—Editorial: "Prejudice against Color," *North Star*, June 13, 1850

I told them that perhaps the greatest hindrance to the adoption of abolition principles by the people of the United States, was the low estimate, everywhere in that country, placed upon the negro, as a man; that because of his assumed natural inferiority, people reconciled themselves to his enslavement and oppression, as things inevitable, if not desirable.

—Autobiography: *My Bondage and My Freedom*, 1855, p. 224

Negro hatred and prejudice of color are . . . merely the offshoots of that root of all crimes and evils—slavery.

—Editorial: "The President and His Speeches," *Douglass' Monthly,*
September 1862

The story of our inferiority is an old dodge, as I have said; for wherever men oppress their fellows, wherever they enslave them, they will
endeavor to find the needed apology for such enslavement and oppression in the character of the people oppressed and enslaved.
—Speech: "What the Black Man Wants?" January 26, 1865,
Douglass Papers, ser. I, 4:65

I was the ugly and deformed child of the family, and to be kept out
of sight as much as possible while there was company in the house.
—Autobiography: *Life and Times,* 1881, p. 305

My color was no longer offensive when it was supposed that I was not
a person, but a piece of property.
—Autobiography: *Life and Times,* 1881, p. 359

If from the cradle through life the outside world brands a class as unfit
for this or that work, the character of the class will come to resemble
and conform to the character described.
—Autobiography: *Life and Times,* 1881, p. 371

The Negro in ignorance and rags meets no resistance. It is only when
he acquires education, property, popularity and influence . . . that he
invites repression.
—Speech: "The Blessings of Liberty and Education," September 3,
1894, *Douglass Papers,* ser. I, 5:628–29

Race Pride
The latent contempt and prejudice towards our race . . . and also the
apparent determination of a portion of the people to hold and treat us

in a degraded relation, not only justify for the present such associate effort on our part, but make it eminently necessary.

—Speech: "The Douglass Institute," September 29, 1865, *Douglass Papers*, ser. I, 4:91

Time, education, and circumstances are rapidly destroying these mere color distinctions, and men will be valued in this country as well as in others, for what they are, and for what they can do.

—Autobiography: *Life and Times*, 1881, p. 322

But the whole assumption of race pride is ridiculous. Let us have done with complexional superiorities or inferiorities, complexional pride or shame. I want no better basis for my activities and affinities than the broad foundation laid by the Bible itself, that God has made of one blood all nations of men to dwell on all the face of the earth.

—Speech: "The Nation's Problem," April 16, 1889, *Douglass Papers*, ser. I, 5:413

Away then with the nonsense that a man must be black to be true to the rights of black men. I put my foot upon the effort to draw lines between white and black or between blacks and so-called Afro-Americans, or race line in the domain of liberty. Whoever is for equal rights, for equal education, for equal opportunities, for all men of whatever race or color, I hail him as a "countryman, clansman, kinsman and brother beloved."

—Speech: "The Blessings of Liberty and Education," September 3, 1894, *Douglass Papers*, ser. I, 5:627

Segregation
[Racial segregation] would make pestilence and pauperism, ignorance and crime, a part of American Institution. . . . The dreadful contagion

of their vices and crimes would fly like cholera and small pox through all classes. Woe, woe! to this land, when it strips five millions of its people of all motives for cultivating an upright character. . . . Do anything with us, but plunge us not into this hopeless pit.

—Editorial: "Future of the Negro People of the Slave States," *Douglass' Monthly*, March 1862

Our legislators, our Presidents, and our judges should have a care, lest, by forcing these people, outside of law, they destroy that love of country which is needful to the nation's defense in the day of trouble.

—Speech: "This Decision Has Humbled the Nation," October 22, 1883, *Douglass Papers*, ser. I, 5:118

A nation within a nation is an anomaly. There can be but one American nation under the American government, and we are Americans.

—Speech: "The Nation's Problem," April 16, 1889, *Douglass Papers*, ser. I, 5:415

The true problem is not the negro, but the nation. Not the law-abiding blacks of the South, but the white men of that section, who by fraud, violence, and persecution, are breaking the law, trampling on the Constitution, corrupting the ballot-box, and defeating the ends of justice. The true problem is whether these white ruffians shall be allowed by the nation to go on in their lawless and nefarious career, dishonoring the Government and making its very name a mockery.

—Speech: "The Negro Problem," October 21, 1890, *Douglass Papers*, ser. I, 5:443–44

Tolerance

It is all false, this talk about the invincibility of prejudice against color. If any of you have it, and no doubt some of you have, I will tell you how to get rid of it. Commence to do something to elevate, and improve and enlighten the colored man, and your prejudice will begin to vanish. The more you try to make a man of the black man, the more you will begin to think him a man.

—Speech: "The Colonizationist Revival," May 31, 1849, *Douglass Papers,* ser. I, 2:213

Men are not valued in this country, or in any country, for what they are; they are valued for what they can do. . . . We must show that we can do as well as be.

—Editorial: "Learn Trades or Starve!" *Frederick Douglass' Paper,* March 4, 1853

Wealth, learning and ability made an Irishman an Englishman. The same metamorphosing power converts a negro into a white man in this country. When prejudice cannot deny the black man's ability, it denies his race, and claims him as a white man.

—Speech: "The Douglass Institute," September 29, 1865, *Douglass Papers,* ser. I, 4:91

I know there is prejudice here; there has always been prejudice. The only way to get rid of your prejudice is to begin to treat the negro as though you had no prejudice, and very soon you will find that you have got none. There is no better way for a man to cure his prejudice than to begin to do good to the victim of that prejudice. The moment you do that, that moment you find your prejudice vanish.

—Speech: "Let the Negro Alone," May 11, 1869, *Douglass Papers,* ser. I, 4:208

I have found in my experience that the way to break down an unreasonable custom, is to contradict it in practice.

—Autobiography: *Life and Times,* 1881, p. 287

If we had built great ships, sailed around the world, taught the science of navigation, discovered far-off islands, capes, and continents,
enlarged the boundaries of human knowledge, improved the conditions of man's existence, brought valuable contributions of art, science,
and literature, revealed great truths, organized great states, administered great governments, defined the laws of the universe, formulated
systems of mental and moral philosophy, invented railroads, steam
engines, mowing machines, sewing machines, taught the sun to take
pictures, the lightning to carry messages, we then might claim, not only
potential and theoretical equality, but actual and practical equality.

    —Speech: "The Nation's Problem," April 16. 1889, *Douglass Papers,*
ser. I, 5:413

I admit that during many years to come the colored man will have to
endure prejudice against his race and color, but this constitutes no problem. The world was never yet without prejudice. . . . But what business
has government, State or National, with these prejudices? Why should
grave statesmen concern themselves with them? The business of government is to hold its broad shield over all and to see that every American
citizen is alike and equally protected in his civil and personal rights.

    —Speech: "The Negro Problem," October 21, 1890, *Douglass
Papers,* ser. I, 5:454–55

Put away your race prejudice. Banish the idea that one class must rule
over another, recognize the fact that the rights of the humblest citizen
are as worthy of protection as are those of the highest, and . . . your
republic will stand and flourish forever.

    —Speech: "Lessons of the Hour," January 9, 1894, *Douglass Papers,*
ser. I, 5:607

Realism

We naturally prefer the bright side, but when there is a dark side it is folly to shut our eyes to it or deny its existence.
—Speech: "The Mission of the War," January 13, 1864, *Douglass Papers*, ser. I, 4:4

Reconstruction
(see also Civil War, Sectional Reconciliation)

Soldiers can capture a State, but statesmen must govern a State. It is sometimes hard to pull down a house but it is always harder to build one up.
—Speech: "The War and How to End It," March 25, 1862, Rochester, N.Y., *Douglass Papers*, ser. I, 3:515

"Let us have peace." Yes, let us have peace, but let us have liberty, law, and justice first. Let us have the Constitution, with its thirteenth, fourteenth, and fifteenth amendments, fairly interpreted, faithfully executed, and cheerfully obeyed in the fullness of their spirit and the completeness of their letter.
—Speech: There Was a Right Side in the Late War," May 30, 1878, *Douglass Papers*, ser. I, 4:485

The thought of paying cash for labor that they could formerly extort by the lash did not in anywise improve their disposition to the emancipated slave, or improve his own condition. Now, since poverty has, and can have no chance against wealth, the landless against the landowner, the ignorant against the intelligent, the freedman was powerless. He had nothing left him but a slavery-distorted and diseased body, and lame and twisted limbs with which to fight the battle of life.

—Autobiography: *Life and Times,* pp. 295–96

Until it shall be safe to leave the lamb in the hold of the lion, the laborer in the power of the capitalist, the poor in the hands of the rich, it will not be safe to leave a newly emancipated people completely in the power of their former masters, especially when such masters have not ceased to be such from enlightened moral convictions but by irresistible force.

—Autobiography: *Life and Times,* 1881, p. 298

Peace with the old master class has been war to the negro.

—Speech: "Our Destiny Is Largely in Our Own Hands," April 16, 1883, *Douglass Papers,* ser. I, 5:61

Reform

All great reforms do together. Whatever tends to elevate, whatever tends to exalt humanity in one portion of the world, tends to exalt it in another part; the same feeling that warms the heart of the philanthropist here, animates that of the lover of humanity in every country.

—Speech: "Intemperance and Slavery," October 20, 1845, *Douglass Papers,* ser. I, 1:58

As one genuine bank bill is worth more than a thousand counterfeits, so is one man, with right on his side, worth more than thousands in the wrong.

—Speech: "The Anti-Slavery Movement," March 18, 1855, *Douglass Papers,* ser. I, 3:49

Let me give you a word of philosophy of reform. The whole history of the progress of human liberty shows that all concessions yet made to her august claims, have been born of earnest struggle. The conflict has been exciting, agitating, all-absorbing, and for the time-being, putting all other tumults to silence. It must do this or it does nothing. If there is no struggle there is no progress. Those who profess to favor freedom and yet depreciate agitation, are men who want crops without plowing up the ground, they want rain without thunder and lightning. They want the ocean without the awful roar of its many waters.

—Speech: "The Significance of Emancipation in the West Indies," August 3, 1857, *Douglass Papers*, ser. I, 3:204

We should never forget, whatever may be the incidental mistakes or misconduct of rulers, that government is better than anarchy, and patient reform is better than violent revolution.

—Autobiography: *Life and Times*, 1881, p. 398

Motives

The man who has thoroughly embraced the principles of Justice, Love, and Liberty, like the true preacher of Christianity is less anxious to reproach the world of its sins, than to win it to repentance. His great work on earth is to exemplify, and to illustrate and to engraft those principles upon the living and practical understandings of all men within the reach of his influence.

—Speech: "The Anti-Slavery Movement," March 18, 1855, *Douglass Papers*, ser. I, 3:45

The mission of the reformer is to discover truth, or the settled and eternal order of the universe.

—Speech: "It Moves," November 20, 1883, *Douglass Papers*, ser. I, 5:142

Tactics

I have no weapon but that which is consistent with morality, I am engaged in a holy war; I ask not the aid of the sword, I appeal to the understanding and the hearts of men—we use these weapons, and hope that God will give us the victory.

—Speech: "The Free States, Slavery, and the Sin of the Free Church," March 19, 1846, *Douglass Papers*, ser. I, 1:187

But sir, I am not here merely because the slave is a man, and I wish you to be interested in him [not] merely because he is a man, but because slavery itself is the common enemy of mankind. If we depend for abolition in the United States upon mere political action, or upon the strong arm, then comes the question as to whether it is expedient for me or anybody else to present the subject to you. But we are not dependent upon the arm of force, for the triumph of our principles—we are not dependent on mere political action for the overthrow of slavery. We are dependent on moral and religious power, that knows no geographical boundaries, that knows no laws, that knows no constitution or forms of government. Wherever one human mind can come in contact with another, this power can be exerted. The slave-holders of America may boast of their ability to throw back ball for ball, bomb-shell for bomb-shell; they may boast of their ability to raise their forts and their ramparts so high as to ward off the strongest blow of a foreign invader; but the truth and light of Christianity, which are moving on the wings of the wind, they can never resist.

—Speech: "Slavery, the Free Church, and British Agitation against Bondage," August 3, 1846, *Douglass Papers*, ser. I, 1:324

It is the voice of all experience that opposition to agitation is the most successful method of promoting it. Men will write—men will read—men will think—men will feel—and the result of this is, men will speak; and it were as well to chain the lightning as to repress the moral convictions and humane promptings of enlightened human nature.

—Speech: "A Nation in the Midst of a Nation," May 11, 1853, *Douglass Papers*, ser. I, 2:436

For men are always disposed to respect and defend rights—when the victims of oppression stand up manfully for themselves.

—Speech: "The Anti-Slavery Movement," March 18, 1855, *Douglass Papers*, ser. I, 3:50

Some men rebuke sin with such manifest levity as only to amuse the sinner. Others denounce wrong as if exulting over the wrong doer, while others show their zeal for truth by stretching it into falsehood and absurdity. All these will offend, disgust, and drive the wrong doer from the teacher or reformer. He will say, your cause may be good, but you are not the man to advocate it.

—Speech: "Eulogy of William Jay," May 12, 1859, *Douglass Papers*, ser. I, 3:275

Religion

A man becomes the more cruel the more the religious element is perverted in him.

—Speech: "Baptists, Congregationalists, the Free Church, and Slavery," December 23, 1845, *Douglass Papers*, ser. I, 1:109

To use a homely expression, I might as well expect to raise myself up by my boot straps as to raise man up looking only to man. I look to God, and in proportion as I get a glimpse of God I embrace Christianity, love God, and love his purity.

—Speech: "Freedom, the Eternal Truth," May 2, 1852, *Douglass Papers*, ser. I, 2:355

I believe in human power; but I believe also in divine power, acting through the nature of things, confounding the wisdom of the crafty, and bringing to nought the councils of the ungodly.
—Speech: "We Are in the Midst of a Moral Revolution," May 19, 1854, *Douglass Papers*, ser. I, 2:482

I found it impossible to respect the religious profession of any who are under the dominion of this wicked prejudice, and I could not, therefore, feel that in joining them, I was joining a christian church, at all.
—Autobiography: *My Bondage and My Freedom*, 1855, p. 203

Organizations are strong, but there is something in the world much stronger than any human organization. The eternal spirit is mightier than all the external world; religion is greater than the form created to express it.
—Speech: "The Anti-Slavery Movement," March 18, 1855, *Douglass Papers*, ser. I, 3:38

I am superstitious enough to believe that the finger of the Almighty may be seen bringing good out of evil, and making the wrath of man redound to his honor, hastening the triumph of righteousness.
—Speech: "The Dred Scott Decision," May 1857, *Douglass Papers*, ser. I, 3:169

The work of the revivalist is more than half done when he has got a man to stand up in the congregation as an indication of his need of grace. The strength of an iron halter—was needed for this first act, but now like Rarey's horses, he may be led by a straw.

—Speech: "Pictures and Progress," December 3, 1861, *Douglass Papers*, ser. I, 3:461

Man everywhere worships man, and in the last analyses worships himself. He finds in himself the qualities he calls divine and reverently bows before them. This is the best he can do. It is the measure of his being. The God of the merciful and just man is merciful and just, despite the Church: and the God of the selfish and cruel man—is a being in wood, stone, iron or in Imagination after his own image, no matter what he has come to believe in the Church Creed.

—Speech: "Pictures and Progress," December 3, 1861, *Douglass Papers*, ser. I, 3:463

[G]enuine goodness is the same, whether found inside or outside the church, and that be an "infidel" no more proves a man to be selfish, mean, and wicked, than to be evangelical proves him to be honest, just, and humane.

—Autobiography: *Life and Times*, 1881, p. 362

[A]ll the prayers of Christendom cannot stop the force of a single bullet, divest arsenic of poison, or suspend any law of nature.

—Autobiography: *Life and Times*, 1881, p. 373

Religious ideas have come to us from the wilderness, from mountain tops, from dens and caves, and from the vast silent spaces from which come the mirage and other shadowy illusions; which create rivers, lakes and forest where there is none.

—Autobiography: *Life and Times*, 1881, p. 429

Proslavery Religion

I love the pure, peaceable and impartial Christianity of Christ:
I therefore hate the corrupt, slaveholding, women-whipping, cradle-
plundering, partial and hypocritical Christianity of this land. Indeed,
I can see no reason, but the most deceitful one, for calling the religion
of this land Christianity. I look upon it as the climax of all misno-
mers, the boldest of all frauds, the grossest of all libels.
    —Autobiography: *Narrative,* 1845, p. 81

The dealers in the bodies and souls of men erect their stand in the
presence of the pulpit, and they mutually help each other. The dealer
gives his blood-stained gold to support the pulpit, and the pulpit, in
return, covers his infernal business with the garb of Christianity. Here
we have religion and robbery the allies of each other; slavery and piety
linked and interlinked; preachers of the gospel united with slaveholders! A horrible sight, to see devils dressed in angels' robes, and hell
presenting the semblance of paradise.
    —Autobiography: *Narrative,* 1845, p. 82

I love religion—I love the religion of Jesus, which is pure and peaceable, and easy to be entreated. I ask you all to love this religion, but
I hate a religion which, in the name of the Saviour, and which pros-
titutes his blessed precepts to the vile purposes of slavery, ruthlessly
sunders all the ties of nature, which tears the wife from the husband—
which separates the child from the parent—which covers the backs of
man and women with bloody scars—which promotes all manner of
licentiousness. I hate such a religion as this, for it not Christianity—it
is of the devil—I ask you to hate it too, and to assist me in putting in
its place the religion of Jesus.
    —Speech: "Irish Christians and Non-Fellowship with Man-
Stealers," October 1, 1845, *Douglass Papers,* ser. I, 1:35

Whatever tends to make slavery respectable, tends to perpetuate it. Well, what have we found making slavery respectable? It is the Free Church of Scotland. The Free Church has attempted to make slaveholders be deemed respectable, and whatever makes the slaveholder respectable, makes the system respectable also.

—Speech: "America's Compromise with Slavery and the Abolitionists' Work," April 6, 1846, *Douglass Papers*, ser. I, I:213

I glory in being called an infidel by a slave-holding church.

—Speech: "Slavery, the Free Church, and British Agitation against Bondage," August 3, 1846, *Douglass Papers*, ser. I, I:328

The very Rev. Chief Priests of our religion, have long the length to assert, that slavery is itself of divine appointment; that in some cases it is a high Christian duty to hold the slave in bondage. . . . They contend that neither Christ nor his apostles ever made slaveholding a barrier to christian fellowship; that Christ and his apostles never did, the church of Christ has no right to do, that it is the duty of the preacher to preach the gospel, to seek the salvation of souls, and never to interfere with the laws and civil arrangements of society, that the latter must be left to the statesman. . . . Thus the church is not only the strongest bulwark of slavery, but it is the point most secure from attack.

—Editorial: "American Religion and American Slavery," *North Star*, June 2, 1850

But a religion which favors the rich against the poor; which exalts the proud above the humble; which divides mankind into two classes, tyrants and slaves; which says to the man in chains, *stay there*; and to the oppressor, *oppress on*; it is a religion which may be professed and enjoyed by all the robbers and enslavers of mankind; it makes God a respecter of persons, denies his fatherhood of the race, and tramples in the dust the great truth of the brotherhood of man.

—Speech: "What to the Slave Is the Fourth of July?" July 5, 1852, *Douglass Papers*, ser. I, 2:378

Roman Catholic Church

Wherever else the Roman Church may question its own strength and practice a modest reserve, here she is open, free, self-asserting and bold in her largest assumptions. She writes indulgences over her gateways as boldly to-day as if Luther had never lived and she jingles the keys of heaven and hell as confidently as if her right to do so had never been called into question.

—Autobiography: *Life and Times*, 1881, p. 423

For whatever may be its other faults and defects, the Roman Catholic church welcomes to its altar and communion men of all races and colors, and would contradict its assumption of being the universal church if it did otherwise.

—Speech: "My Foreign Travels," December 15, 1887, *Douglass Papers*, ser. I, 5:302

Scriptures

The unity of the human race—the brotherhood of man—the reciprocal duties of all to each, and of each to all, are too plainly taught in the Bible to admit of cavil. The credit of the Bible is at stake—and if it be too much to say that it must stand or fall by the decision of this question, *it is* proper to say, that the value of that sacred Book—as a record of the early history of mankind—must be materially affected, by the decision of the question.

—Speech: "The Claims of the Negro Ethnologically Considered," July 12, 1854, *Douglass Papers*, ser. I, 2:505

Segregation

We held our meeting in an old fashioned, odd shaped meeting-house, owned, I believe, by the town—one reason why we got it, perhaps. It was built in 1804, and bears upon it marks of the negro-hating religion it was built to promote. Upon entering the house, I was pointed, to a hole left in the wall about twelve feet long, on the right hand side of the pulpit. For a time, I was at a loss to know for what it was intended. I got friend White to ask an old gentleman, whom I supposed to be a resident of the place, what the hole was for. He answered very promptly, "It was what they called a nigger's seat." I immediately made my way up to it. I had to go out of the house to find the stair-way—I ought to say, the ladder-way, leading to it. But for the sexton, who kindly offered to conduct me, I should have had greatly difficulty in finding it. With his assistance, after many windings up the steps, I was ushered into this hole, peeping over the side of which, I had a commanding view of nearly all parts of the house. So high was I above the rest, my head became dizzy as I gazed down upon them. I soon descended from my lofty elevation, and gave place to our friends, the Hutchinsons, who took possession of the "nigger pew." They broke upon us with one of their most inspiring songs, in condemnation of the unhallowed prejudice against color existing in that town, as indicated by the pew they then occupied. The audience, with amazement, gazed up to the place from whence the heavenly melody emanated, and, for a moment, stood charmed by the enchanting sounds; at the close of which, they shook the old house with applause. The minister of the church, worshipping in the house, took early opportunity to inform us, that the pew in question had gone out of use—that colored people could now sit where they pleased; another evidence of the progress of our cause.

—Correspondence: Douglass to William Lloyd Garrison, March 6, 1844, *Douglass Papers*, ser. 3, 1:20–21

Skepticism

Forever would we prefer the fellowship of the skeptic who recognizes us as men to the devout saint who can only regard us . . . as excluded from the dignity of humanity; Forever commend us to a sound man in preference to a rotten religionist.

—Editorial: "Slaveholding Religion," *Douglass' Monthly*, October 1860

Tolerance

Of all motives for persecution, the blindest and most bitter is that which falsely calls itself religion.

—Editorial: "The American Religion and American Slavery," *North Star*, June 27, 1850

I know of no church, however tolerant; of no priesthood however enlightened, which could be safely trusted with the tremendous power which universal conformity would confer. We should welcome all men of every shade of religious opinion, as among the best means of checking the arrogance and intolerance which are the almost inevitable concomitants of general conformity. Religious liberty always flourishes best amid the clash and competition of rival religious creeds.

—Speech: "Our Composite Nationality," December 7, 1869, *Douglass Papers*, ser. I, 4:258

There is, worst of all, religious prejudice, a prejudice which has stained whole continents with blood. It is, in fact, a spirit infernal, against which every enlightened man should wage perpetual war.

—Autobiography: *Life and Times*, 1881, p. 401

Resignation

A man's troubles are always half disposed of, when he finds endurance his only remedy.
—Autobiography: *My Bondage and My Freedom*, 1855, p. 39

Respect

Strange, and even ridiculous as it may seem, among a people so uncultivated, and with so many stern trials to look in the face, there is not to be found, among any people, a more rigid enforcement of the law of respect to elders, than they [slaves] maintain.
—Autobiography: *My Bondage and My Freedom*, 1855, p. 41

The claim of our fathers upon our memory, admiration and gratitude, are founded in the fact that they wisely, and bravely, and successfully met the crisis of their day. And if the men of this generation would deserve well of posterity they must like their fathers, discharge the duties and responsibilities of their age.
—Speech: "The Slaveholders' Rebellion," July 4, 1862, *Douglass Papers*, ser. I, 3:523

A man must be low indeed when he does not want someone below him.
—Speech: "Our Composite Nationality," December 7, 1869, *Douglass Papers*, ser. I, 4:251

Revolution

The thing worse than rebellion is the thing that causes rebellion.
—Essay: "Reconstruction," *Atlantic Monthly* 18 (1866): 761–65

The ideas of a common humanity against privileged classes, of common rights against special privileges, are now rocking the world.
—Speech: "Our Destiny Is Largely in Our Own Hands," April 16, 1883, *Douglass Papers*, ser. I, 5:67

All the world is a school, and in it one lesson is just now being taught in letters of fire and blood, and that is, the utter insecurity of life and property in the presence of an aggrieved class.
—Speech: "We Are Confronted by a New Administration," April 16, 1885, *Douglass Papers*, ser. I, 5:187

Sectional Reconciliation
(see also Civil War, Reconstruction)

The imperfections of memory, the multitudinous throngs of events, the fading effects of time upon the national mind, and the growing affection of the loyal nation for the late rebels, will, on the page of our national history, obscure the negro's part, though they can never blot it out entirely, nor can it be entirely forgotten.
—Autobiography: *Life and Times*, 1881, p. 381

The country had not quite survived the effects and influence of its great war for existence. The serpent had been wounded but not killed. Under the disguise of meekly accepting the results and decisions of the war, the rebels had come back to Congress more with the pride of conquerors than with the repentant humility of defeated traitors.
—Autobiography: *Life and Times*, 1881, p. 384

Self-Awareness

Men seldom see themselves as other see them. . . .
  —Autobiography: *My Bondage and My Freedom,* 1855, p. 158

There are moments in the lives of most men, when the doors of their souls are open, and unconsciously to themselves, their true characters may be read by the observant eye.
  —Autobiography: *Life and Times,* 1881, p. 285

Self-Defense

[T]here are times when such defense is a privilege to be exercised or omitted at the pleasure of the party assailed, there are other times and circumstances when it becomes a duty which cannot be omitted without the imputation of cowardice or of conscious guilt.
  —Autobiography: *Life and Times,* 1881, p. 442

Slaveholders

That cheerful eye, under the influence of slavery, eventually became red with rage; that voice, made all of sweet accord, changed to one of harsh and horrid discord; and that angelic face gave place to that of a demon. Thus is slavery the enemy of the slave and the slaveholder.
  —Autobiography: *Narrative,* 1845, p. 31

The slave is a subject, subjected by others; the slaveholder is a subject, but he is the author of his own subjugation.
  —Autobiography: *My Bondage and My Freedom,* 1855, p. 62

I want the slave-holder surrounded, as by a wall of anti-slavery fire, so that he may see the condemnation of himself and his system glaring down in letters of light. I want him to feel that he has no sympathy in England, Scotland, or Ireland; that he has none in Canada, none in Mexico, none among the poor wild Indians; that the voice of the civilised aye, and savage world is against him. I would have condemnation blaze down upon him in every direction, till, stunned and overwhelmed with shame and confusion, he is compelled to let go the grasp he holds upon the persons of his victims, and restore them to their long-lost rights.

—Speech: "England Should Lead the Cause of Emancipation," December 23, 1846, *Douglass Papers*, ser. I, 1:481

The Slaveholder is not satisfied to associate with men in the Church or in the State, unless he can thereby stain them with the blood of his Slaves. To be a Slaveholder, is to be a propagandist from necessity; for Slavery can only live by keeping down the under-growth morality which nature supplies.

—Speech: "The Anti-Slavery Movement," March 19, 1855, *Douglass Papers*, ser. I, 3:50

No man is really free south of the Mason & Dixon Line but the slave-holder. And soon no man north of the Mason & Dixon Line will be free but him who will succumb to the demands of the slaveholder.

—Speech: "The Encroachment of the Slave Power," September 5, 1855, *Douglass Papers*, ser. I, 3:100

Character
[W]hen I made him six dollars, sometimes [he] give me six cents, to encourage me. . . . I regarded it as a sort of admission of my right to the whole. The fact that he gave me any part of my wages was proof,

to my mind, that he believed me entitled to the whole of them. I always felt worse for having received anything; for I feared that the giving me a few cents would ease his conscience, and make him feel himself to be a pretty honorable sort of robber.

—Autobiography: *Narrative*, 1845, pp. 71–72

Slaves are not insensible to the whole-souled characteristics of a generous, dashing slaveholder, who is fearless of consequences; and they prefer a master of this bold and daring kind—even with the risk of being shot down for impudence—to the fretful, little soul, who never uses the lash but at the suggestion of a love of gain.

—Autobiography: *My Bondage and My Freedom*, 1855, p. 39

Under the whole heavens there is no relation more unfavorable to the development of honorable character, than that sustained by the slaveholder to the slave. Reason is imprisoned here, and passions run wild. Like the fires of the prairie, once lighted, they are at the mercy of every wind, and must burn till they have consumed all that is combustible within their remorseless grasp.

—Autobiography: *My Bondage and My Freedom*, 1855, p. 47

Religious slaveholders, like religious persecutors, are ever extreme in their malice and violence.

—Autobiography: *My Bondage and My Freedom*, 1855, p. 148

But the kindness of the slavemaster only gilds the chains of slavery, and detracts nothing from its weight or power.

—Autobiography: *My Bondage and My Freedom*, 1855, p. 155

Reputation

It [witnessing a slave-whipping] struck me with awful force. It was the blood-stained gate, the entrance to the hell of slavery, through which

I was about to pass. It was a most terrible spectacle. I wish I could commit to paper the feelings with which I beheld it.

—Autobiography: *Narrative*, 1845, p. 16

It was considered as being bad enough to be a slave; but to be a poor man's slave was deemed a disgrace indeed!

—Autobiography: *Narrative*, 1845, p. 24

Every city slaveholder is anxious to have it known of him, that he feeds his slaves well; and it is due to them to say, that most of them do give their slaves enough to eat.

—Autobiography: *Narrative*, 1845, 32

Violence

The truth was being told, and having its legitimate effect upon the hearts of those who heard it. At last . . . the slaveholders, convinced that reason, morality, common honesty, humanity, and Christianity, were all against them, and that argument was no longer any means of defense, or at least but a poor means, abandoned their post . . . and resorted to their old and natural mode of defending their morality by brute force.

—Correspondence: Douglass to William Lloyd Garrison, September 1, 1845, *Douglass Papers*, ser. 3, 1:46

Slavery

Slaveholders and slave-traders never betray greater indiscretion, than when they venture to defend themselves, or their system of plunder, in any other community than a slaveholding one. Slavery has its own standard of morality, humanity, justice, and Christianity.

Tried by that standard, it is a system of the greatest kindness to the slave—sanctioned by the purest morality—in perfect agreement with justice—and, of course, not inconsistent with Christianity. But, tried by any other, it is doomed to condemnation. The naked relation of master and slave is one of those monsters of darkness, to whom the light of truth is death! The wise ones among slaveholders know this, and they studiously avoid doing anything, which, in their judgment, tends to elicit truth. They seem fully to understand, that their safety is in their silence.

—Correspondence: Douglass to William Lloyd Garrison, January 27, 1846, *Douglass Papers*, ser. 3, 1:82

Slavery blunts the edge of all of our rebukes of tyranny abroad—the criticisms that we make upon other nations only call forth ridicule, contempt, and scorn. In a word, we are made a reproach and a by-word to the mocking earth, and we must continue to be made so, so long as slavery continues to pollute our soil.

—Speech: "An Anti-Slavery Tocsin," December 8, 1850, *Douglass Papers*, ser. I, 2:269–70

Slavery aims at ultimate sway and to banish liberty from the republic. It would drive out the schoolmaster and install the slave-driver, burn the schoolhouse and install the whipping post, prohibit the Holy Bible and establish the bloody slave code, dishonor free labor with its hope of reward, and establish slave labor with its dread of the lash.

—Editorial: "Present Condition and Future Prospects," *Frederick Douglass' Paper*, February 24, 1854

Nature has done almost nothing to prepare men and women to be either slaves or slaveholders. Nothing but rigid training, long persisted in, can perfect the character of the one or the other. One cannot easily forget to love freedom; and it is as hard to cease to respect that natural love in our fellow creatures.

—Autobiography: *My Bondage and My Freedom*, 1855, p. 87

What was slavery? A standing insurrection from beginning to end—a perpetual chronic insurrection.

—Speech: "John Brown and the Slaveholders' Insurrection," January 30, 1860, *Douglass Papers*, ser. I, 3:317

Evils of Slavery

The existence of slavery in this country brands your republicanism as a sham, your humanity as a base pretense, and your Christianity as a lie. It destroys your moral power abroad; it corrupts your politicians at home. It saps the foundation of religion; it makes your name a hissing, and a by-word to a mocking earth. It is the antagonistic force in your government, the only thing that seriously disturbs and endangers your *Union*. It fetters your progress; it is the enemy of improvement, the deadly foe of education; it fosters pride; it breeds insolence; it promotes vice; it shelters crime; it is a curse to the earth that supports it; and yet, you cling to it, as if it were the sheet anchor of all your hopes. Oh! be warned! be warned! a horrible reptile is coiled up in your nation's bosom; the venomous creature is nursing at the tender breast of your youthful republic; *for the love of God, tear away,* and fling from you the hideous monster, and *let the weight of twenty millions crush and destroy it forever!*

—Speech: "What to the Slave Is the Fourth of July?" July 5, 1852, *Douglass Papers*, ser. I, 2:383–84

The evils most fostered by slavery and oppression are precisely those which slaveholders and oppressors would transfer from their system to the inherent character of their victims. Thus the very crimes of slavery become slavery's best defense. By making the enslaved a character fit only for slavery, they excuse themselves for refusing to make the slave a freeman.

—Speech: "The Claims of the Negro Ethnologically Considered," July 12, 1854, *Douglass Papers,* ser. I, 2:507

Manumission

The highest evidence the slaveholder can give the slave of his acceptance with God, is the emancipation of his slaves. This is proof that he is willing to give up all to God, and for the sake of God. Not to do this, was, in my estimation, and in the opinion of all the slaves, an evidence of half-heartedness, and wholly inconsistent with the idea of genuine conversion.

—Autobiography: *My Bondage and My Freedom,* 1855, p. 112

Reparations

What class of people can show a better title to the land on which they live than the colored people of the South? They have . . . produced whatever had made it a goodly land to dwell in, and it would be a shame and a crime little inferior in enormity to Slavery itself if these natural owners of the Southern and Gulf States should be driven away from their country.

—Editorial: "Future of the Negro People of the Slave States," *Douglass' Monthly,* March 1862

People who live now, and talk of doing too much for the Negro . . . forget that for all of these terrible wrongs there is, in truth, no redress and no adequate compensation. The enslaved and battered millions have come, suffered, died and gone with all of their moral and physical wounds into Eternity. To them no recompense can be made. If the American people could put a school house in every valley; a church on every hill top in the South and supply them with a teacher and preacher respectively and welcome the descendants of the former slaves to all the moral and intellectual benefits of the one and the other . . . such a sacrifice would not compensate their children for the terrible wrong done to their father and mother.

—Speech: "The Blessings of Liberty and Education," September 3, 1894, *Douglass Papers*, ser. 1, 5:624

Slaves

Character

Experience proves that those are oftenest abused who can be abused with the greatest impunity. They prefer to whip those who are most easily whipped. The old doctrine that submission is the best cure for outrage and wrong, does not hold good on the slave plantation. He is whipped oftenest, who is whipped easiest; and that slave who has the courage to stand up for himself against the overseer, although he may have many stripes at the first, becomes, in the end, a freeman, even though he sustain the formal relation of a slave.

—Autobiography: *My Bondage and My Freedom*, 1855, pp. 55–56

The allotments of Providence seem to make the black man of America the open book out of which the American people are to learn lessons of wisdom, power, and goodness—more sublime and glorious than any yet attained by the nations of old or the new world. Over the bleeding back of the American bondsman we shall learn mercy. In the very extreme difference of color and features of the Negro and the Anglo-Saxon, shall be learned the highest ideas of sacredness of man and the fullness and perfection of human brotherhood.

—Editorial: "Future of the Negro People of the Slave States," *Douglass' Monthly*, March 1862

Discontent

[A] deep conviction that slavery would not always be able to hold me within its foul embrace; and in the darkest hours of my career in slavery, this living word of faith and spirit of hope departed not from me, but remained like ministering angels to cheer me through the gloom.

—Autobiography: *Narrative*, 1845, p. 30

I have observed this in my experience of slavery,—that whenever my condition was improved, instead of it increasing my contentment, it only increased my desire to be free, and set me to thinking of plans to gain my freedom. I have found that, to make a contented slave, it is necessary to make a thoughtless one. It is necessary to darken his moral and mental vision, and, as far as possible, to annihilate the power of reason. He must be able to detect no inconsistencies in slavery; he must be made to feel that slavery is right; and he can be brought to that only when he ceases to be a man.

—Autobiography: *Narrative*, 1845, p. 70

The wretchedness of slavery, and the blessedness of freedom, were perpetually before me. It was life and death to me.

—Autobiography: *Narrative*, 1845, p. 74

[Slave power's depredations have stirred] among the colored people . . . a spirit of manly resistance well calculated to surround them with a bulwark of sympathy and respect hitherto unknown.

—Speech: "The Anti-Slavery Movement," March 19, 1855, *Douglass Papers*, ser. I, 3:50

Beat and cuff your slave, keep him hungry and spiritless, and he will follow the chain of his master like a dog; but, feed and clothe him well,—work him moderately—surround him with physical comfort,—and dreams of freedom intrude. Give him a *bad* master, and he aspires to a *good* master; give him a good master, and he wishes to become his *own* master. Such is human nature. You may hurl a man so low, beneath the level of his kind, that he loses all just ideas of his natural position; but elevate him a little, and the clear conception of rights rises to life and power, and leads him onward.

 —Autobiography: *My Bondage and My Freedom,* 1855, p. 150

To make a contented slave, you must make a thoughtless one. It is necessary to darken his moral and mental vision, and, as far as possible, to annihilate his power of reason. He must be able to detect no inconsistencies in slavery. The man that takes his earnings, must be able to convince him that he has the perfect right to do so. It must not depend upon mere force; the slave must know no Higher Law than his master's will. The whole relationship must not only demonstrate, to his mind, its necessity, but its absolute rightfulness. If there be one crevice through which a single drop may fall, it will certainly rust off the slave's chains.

 —Autobiography: *My Bondage and My Freedom,* 1855, p. 183

Escapes

On the one hand, there stood slavery, a stern reality, glaring frightfully upon us,—its robes already crimsoned with the bloods of millions, and even now feasting itself greedily upon our own flesh. On the other hand, away back in the dim distance, under the flickering light of the north star, behind some craggy hill or snow-covered mountain, stood a doubtful freedom—half frozen—beckoning us to come and share its hospitality.

 —Autobiography: *Narrative,* 1845, p. 61

Family

But it is in harmony with the grand aim of slavery, which, always and everywhere, is to reduce man to a level with the brute. It is a successful method of obliterating from the mind and heart of the slave, all just ideas of the sacredness of *the family*, as an institution.

—Autobiography: *My Bondage and My Freedom*, 1855, p. 22

Brothers and sisters we were by blood; but slavery had made us strangers. I heard the words brothers and sisters, and knew they must mean something; but slavery had robbed these terms of their true meaning.

—Autobiography: *My Bondage and My Freedom*, 1855, p. 29

Slavery has no use for either fathers or families, and its laws do not recognize their existence in the social arrangements of the plantation.

—Autobiography: *My Bondage and My Freedom*, 1855, p. 31

A man who will enslave his own blood, may not be safely relied on for magnanimity. Men do not love those who remind them of their sins—unless they have a mind to repent—and the mulatto child's face is a standing accusation against him who is master and father to the child.

—Autobiography: *My Bondage and My Freedom*, 1855, p. 35

Morality

[I]t is one of the damning characteristics of the slave system, that it robs its victims of every earthly incentive to a holy life.

—Autobiography: *My Bondage and My Freedom*, 1855, p. 50

The morality of *free* society can have no application to *slave* society. Slaveholders have made it almost impossible for the slave to commit any crime, known either to the laws of God or to the laws of man.

If he steals, he takes his own; if he kills his master, he imitates only the heroes of the revolution. Slaveholders I hold to be individually and collectively responsible for all the evils which grow out of the horrid relation, and I believe they will be so held at the judgment, in the sight of a just God. Make a man a slave, and you rob him of moral responsibility.

—Autobiography: *My Bondage and My Freedom,* 1855, p. 109

Rebellions

But though my blood still burns, and my heart bounds as I look back to those dark days of slavery, I would rather at this moment exchange places with the veriest whipped slave of the South, than the wealthiest slaveholder of the region. He can have no peace. His mind must be constantly casting up mire and dirt. You can see him gather up his bowie-knife and revolver and place them under his pillow at night. That bowie-knife is intended to pierce the heart of the slave, and that revolver to scatter his brains to the four winds of Heaven. But they first pierce the heart of the slave owner's happiness, and scatter his peace to the winds, ere they reach the poor slave. The slaveholder can know no peace.

—Speech: "The Encroachment of the Slave Power," September 5, 1855, *Douglass Papers,* ser. I, 3:103

After resisting him [Edward Covey], I felt as I had never felt before. It was a resurrection from the dark and pestiferous tomb of slavery, to the heaven of comparative freedom. I was no longer a servile coward, trembling under the form of a brother worm of the dust, but, my long-cowed spirit was roused to an attitude of manly independence. I had reached the point, at which I was *not afraid to die.* This spirit made me a freeman in *fact,* while I remained a slave in *form.*

—Autobiography: *My Bondage and My Freedom,* 1855, p. 141

The slaveholder, kind or cruel, is a slaveholder still—the every hour violator of the just and inalienable rights of man; and he is, therefore, every hour silently whetting the knife of vengeance for his own throat. He never lisps a syllable in commendation of the fathers of this republic, nor denounces any attempted oppression of himself, without inviting the knife to his own throat, and asserting the rights of rebellion for his own slaves.

—Autobiography: *My Bondage and My Freedom*, 1855, pp. 153–54

Again, I am aware that the insurrectionary movements of the slaves were held by many to be prejudicial to their cause. This is said now of such movement at the South. The answer is that abolition followed close on the heels of insurrection in the West Indies, and Virginia was never nearer emancipation than when General Turner kindled the fires of insurrection at Southampton.

—Speech: "The Significance of Emancipation in the West Indies," August 3, 1857, *Douglass Papers*, ser. I, 3:207–8

Outside philanthropy never disenthralled any people. It required a Spartacus . . . to arouse the servile population of Italy, and defeat some of the most powerful armies of Rome, at the head of an army of slaves, and the slaves of America await the advent of an American Spartacus.

—Editorial: *Douglass' Monthly*, April 1860

Songs
The singing of a man cast away upon a desolate island might be as appropriately considered as evidence of contentment and happiness, as the singing of the slave; the songs of the one and the other are prompted by the same emotion.

—Autobiography: *Narrative*, 1845, p. 21

Slaves sing more to make themselves happy, than to express their happiness.

—Autobiography: *My Bondage and My Freedom*, 1855, p. 58

Treatment

No man could assert over another the right of property—he was free to act—free to go and free to come; but the slave was bound in unending chains—he could not improve, progress was annihilated in him.

—Speech: "Slavery as It Now Exists in the United States," August 25, 1846, *Douglass Papers*, ser. I, 1:345

[The] question is one in which white men, as well as black men, are immediately interested. . . . Slavery invades the rights of man, irrespective of color and condition.

—Editorial: "The Doom of the Black Power," *Frederick Douglass' Paper*, July 27, 1855

Ignorance is a high virtue in human chattel; and as the master studies to keep the slave ignorant, the slave is cunning enough to make the master think he succeeds.

—Autobiography: *My Bondage and My Freedom*, 1855, p. 48

Sleep

There is a healing in the angel wing of sleep, even for the slave-boy; and its balm was never more welcome to any wounded soul than it was to mine, the first night I spent at the domicile of my old master.

—Autobiography: *My Bondage and My Freedom*, 1855, p. 30

SLEEP itself does not always come to the relief of the weary in body, and the broken in spirit; especially when past troubles only foreshadow coming disasters.

—Autobiography: *My Bondage and My Freedom,* 1855, p. 133

Success

All human experience proves over and over again, that any success which comes through meanness, trickery, fraud and dishonor, is but emptiness and will only be a torment to its possessor.

—Speech: "Self-Made Men," March 1893, *Douglass Papers,* ser. I, 5:561

Suffrage
(see also Civil Rights, Constitution)

Shall we at this moment justify the deprivation of the negro of the right to vote because some one else is deprived of their privilege? I hold that women as well as men have the right to vote, and my heart and my voice go with the movement to extend suffrage to women.

—Speech: "What the Black Man Wants?" January 26, 1865, *Douglass Papers,* ser. I, 4:62–63

Blacks
It is said that the colored man is ignorant, and therefore he shall not vote. In saying this, you lay down a rule for the black man that you apply to no other class of your citizens. I will hear nothing of degradation nor of ignorance against the black man. If he knows enough to be hanged, he knows enough to vote. If he knows an honest man

from a thief, he knows much more than some of our white voters. If he knows as much when sober as an Irishman knows when drunk, he knows enough to vote. If he knows enough to take up arms in defense of this government, and bare his breast to the storm of rebel artillery, he knows enough to vote.

—Speech: "Emancipation, Racism, and the Work before Us," December 4, 1863, *Douglass Papers*, ser. 3, 3:604

In a republican country where general suffrage is the rule, without the ballot personal liberty and other foregoing rights become mere privileges held at the option of others.

—Speech: "Address to the National Convention of Colored Men Held in Syracuse, New York," October 4–7, 1864, in Quarles, *Frederick Douglass*, p. 217

If the negro knows enough to pay taxes, he knows enough to vote; if the negro can form an opinion respecting the claims of rival candidates and parties, and knows good from evil, as all your laws concerning his conduct imply, he knows enough to vote. If he knows enough to commit crime and to be hanged or imprisoned, he knows enough to vote. If he knows enough to fight for his country when assailed by invasion from abroad, or rebellion at home, he knows enough to vote. Talk not of his ignorance, degradation and servility, he is a man, and if he knows as much when sober, as an Irishman knows when drunk, he knows enough to vote on long established American usage.

—Speech: "A Friendly Word to Maryland," November 17, 1864, *Douglass Papers*, ser. I, 4:49–50

It is said that we are ignorant; I admit it. But if we know enough to be hung, we know enough to vote. If the negro knows enough to pay taxes to support the Government, he knows enough to vote—taxation and representation should go together. If he knows enough to shoulder a musket and fight for the flag, fight for the Government, he knows enough to vote. If he knows as much when he is sober as an Irishman knows when drunk, he knows enough to vote, on good American principles.

—Speech: "What the Black Man Wants?" January 26, 1865, *Douglass Papers*, ser. I, 4:66

Slavery is not abolished until the black man has the ballot. While the Legislatures of the South retain the right to pass laws making any discrimination between black and white, slavery still lives there.

—Speech: "In What New Skin Will the Old Snake Come Forth?" May 10, 1865, *Douglass Papers*, ser. I, 4:83

The American people are bound—bound by their sense of honor (I hope by their sense of honor, at least by a just sense of honor) to extend the franchise to the negro, and I was going to say, that the Abolitionists of the American Anti-Slavery Society were bound to "stand still and see the salvation of God," until that work is done. Where, where shall the black man look for that support, my friends, if the American Anti-Slavery Society fails him.

—Speech: "In What New Skin Will the Old Snake Come Forth?" May 10, 1865, *Douglass Papers*, ser. I, 4:84

If the elective franchise is not extended to the negro, he dies—he is exterminated.

—Speech: "Women's Rights Are Not Inconsistent with Negro Rights," November 19, 1868, *Douglass Papers*, ser. I, 4:183

I insisted that there was no safety for him, or for anybody else in America, outside the American government: that to guard, protect, and maintain his liberty, the freedman should have the ballot; that the liberties of the American people were dependent upon the Ballot-box, the Jury-box, and the Cartridge-box, that without these no class of people could live and flourish in this country, and this was now the word for the hour with me, and the word to which the people of the north willingly listened when I spoke. Hence, regarding as I did, the elective franchise as the one great power by which all civil rights are obtained, enjoyed, and maintained under our form of government, and the one without which freedom to any class is delusive if not impossible, I set myself to work with whatever force and energy I possessed to secure this power for the recently emancipated millions.

—Autobiography: *Life and Times*, 1881, p. 296

The proposition to disenfranchise the colored voter of the South in order to solve the race problem I hereby denounce as a mean and cowardly proposition, utterly unworthy of an honest, truthful and grateful nation. It is a proposition to sacrifice friends in order to conciliate enemies; to surrender the constitution to the late rebels for the lack of moral courage to execute its provisions.

—Speech: "Lessons of the Hour," January 9, 1894, *Douglass Papers*, ser. I, 5:595

Women

All that distinguishes man as an intelligent and accountable being, is equally true of woman; and if that government is only just which governs by the free consent of the governed, there can be no reason in the world for denying to woman the exercise of the elective franchise, or a hand in making and administering the laws of the land.

—Editorial: "The Rights of Women," *North Star*, July 28, 1848

He demanded the ballot for woman because she is a citizen, because she is subjected to the laws, because she is taxed, and because, if she commits crime, she is subject to the laws, because she is convicted and punished like any other criminal. If we admit women to be a reasoning and responsible being, we admit the whole. Woman must be harmoniously educated, and nothing but the ballot will give her an adequate knowledge of politics. Then she shall have the light of her intellect and the benefit of her remarkable intuition in our public affairs. In matters of criticism he felt more confidence in a woman of good sense and taste than in any man. Let woman go to the polls and express her will, and we shall have different men and measures than we have now.

—Speech: "Let No One Be Excluded from the Ballot Box," November 20, 1866, *Douglass Papers*, ser. I, 4:148

Plainly enough, woman has a heavy grievance in being denied the exercise of the elective franchise. She is taxed without representation, tried without a jury of her peers, governed without her consent, and punished for violating laws she has had no hand in making.

—Speech: "Who and What Is Woman?" May 24, 1886, *Douglass Papers*, ser. I, 5:254

I have never yet been able to find one consideration, one argument, or suggestion in favor of man's right to participate in civil government which did not equally apply to the right of woman.

—Autobiography: *Life and Times*, 1881, p. 371

[W]oman's cause is already a brilliant success. But, however this may be, and whatever the future may have in store for us, one thing is certain—this new revolution in human thought will never go backward. When a great truth once gets abroad in the world, no power on earth can imprison it, or prescribe its limits, or suppress it. It is bound to go on till it becomes the thought of the world.

—Speech: "Give Women Fair Play," March 31, 1888, *Douglass Papers*, ser. I, 5:355

But, as I understand the matter, woman does not ask man for the right of suffrage. That is something which man has no power to give. Rights do not have their source in the will or the grace of man. They are not such things as he can grant or withhold according to his sovereign will and pleasure. All that woman can properly ask man to do in this case, and all that man can do, is get out of the way, and let woman express her sentiments at the polls and in the government, equally with himself. Give her fair play and let her alone.

—Speech: "I Am a Radical Woman Suffrage Man," May 28, 1888, *Douglass Papers*, ser. I, 5:383

But if, on the contrary, human nature is more virtuous than vicious, as I believe it is, if governments are best supported by the largest measure of virtue within their reach, if women are equally virtuous with men, if the whole is greater than a part, if the sense and sum of human goodness in man and woman combined is greater than in that of either alone and separate, then the government that excludes women from all participation in its creation, administration and perpetuation, maims itself, deprives itself of one-half of all that is wisest and best for its usefulness, success and perfection.

—Speech: "I Am a Radical Woman Suffrage Man," May 28, 1888, *Douglass Papers*, ser. I, 5:387

Tariffs

[T]he principle of self protection taught in every department of nature whether in men, beasts or plants. It comes with the inherent right to exist. It is in every blade of grass as well as in every man and nation. If foreign manufactures oppress and cripple ours and serve to retard our natural progress, we have the right to protect ourselves against such efforts.

—Autobiography: *Life and Times*, 1881, p. 438

Time

Time itself is a conservative power—a very conservative power. One shake of his hoary locks will sometimes paralyze the hand and palsy the tongue of the reformer.

—Speech: "Give Women Fair Play," March 31, 1888, *Douglass Papers*, ser. I, 5:354

Travel

Man is by Nature a migratory animal. It does not appear that he was intended to dwell forever in any one locality. He is a born traveler.

—Speech: "My Foreign Travels," December 15, 1887, *Douglass Papers*, ser. I, 5:279

The fact is the measure and value of what a man brings from abroad depends largely upon the amount and value of what he takes from home.

—Speech: "My Foreign Travels," December 15, 1887, *Douglass Papers*, ser. I, 5:283

Egyptian Pyramids

There they stand, however, grandly, in sight of Cairo, just in the edge of the Libyan desert and overlooking the valley of the Nile, as they have stood during more than three thousand years and are likely to stand as many thousand years longer, for nothing grows old here but time and that lives on forever.

—Autobiography: *Life and Times*, 1881, p. 431

Mediterranean Sea

[T]he blue and tideless waters of the Mediterranean, a sea charming in itself and made more charming by the poetry and eloquence it has inspired.

—Autobiography: *Life and Times*, 1881, p. 417

Roman Coliseum

No building more elaborate, vast and wonderful than this has risen since the Tower of Babel.

—Autobiography: *Life and Times*, 1881, p. 422

St. Peter's Cathedral

It is hard to imagine any structure built by human hands more grand and imposing than this dome as seen from the Pincian Hill, especially near the sunset hour. Towering high above the ample body of the great Cathedral and the world famed Vatican, it is bathed in a sea of ethereal glory. Its magnificence and impressiveness gain by distance. When you move away from it, it seems to follow you, and though you travel fast and far, when you look back it will be there and more impressive than ever.

—Autobiography: *Life and Times*, 1881, p. 424

Trust

Mankind are not held together by lies. Trust is the foundation of society. Where there is no truth, there can be no trust, and where there is no trust, there can be no society. Where there is society, there is trust, and where there is trust, there is something upon which it is supported.

—Speech: "Our Composite Nationality," December 7, 1869, *Douglass Papers*, ser. I, 4:257

Truth

It will be time enough to utter new truths, when the old ones are admitted.

—Speech: "Principles of Temperance Reform," March 5, 1848, *Douglass Papers*, ser. I, 2:107

It is a poor rule that won't work both ways.

—Speech: "The Colonizationist Revival," May 31, 1849, *Douglass Papers*, ser. I, 2:214

The only power, worth a snap of your finger is the POWER OF TRUTH. Truth is the power of God; the power of God unto salvation. The good lever of the Almighty, to raise man from Slavery to freedom, from ignorance to intelligence, from vice to virtue.

—Speech: "Is the Constitution Pro-Slavery?" January 27, 1850, *Douglass Papers*, ser. I, 2:232–33

There are times in the experience of almost every community, when even the humblest member thereof may properly presume to teach—when the wise and great ones, the appointed leaders of the people, exert their powers of mind to complicate, mystify, entangle and obscure the simple truth—when they exert the noblest gifts which heaven has vouchsafed to man to mislead the popular mind, and to corrupt the public heart,—then the humblest may stand forth and be excused for opposing even his weakness to the torrent of evil.

—Speech: "Slavery and the Slave Power," December 1, 1850, *Douglass Papers*, ser. I, 2:250

There are two methods of dealing with false and dangerous theories and practices among men; and both have their uses. ONE is, to denounce, in strong and burning words, such theories and practices; and this is the shortest, easiest and commonest. The other is, to illustrate and expose, by a careful analysis, all the facts and particulars, pertaining to such theories and practices; and this is the least usual, because the most difficult method of the two.

—Speech: "Henry Clay and Colonization Rant, Sophistry, and Falsehood," February 2, 1851, *Douglass Papers*, ser. I, 2:314

Error may be new or it may be old, since it is founded in a misapprehension of what truth is. It has its beginnings and has its endings. But not so with truth. Truth is eternal. Like the great God from whose throne it emanates, it is from everlasting unto everlasting, and can never pass away.

—Speech: "Slavery, Freedom, and the Kansas-Nebraska Act," October 30, 1854, *Douglass Papers*, ser. I, 2:558

Truth is mighty, and will prevail . . . is a *maxim,* which we do not regard as a mere rhetorical flourish.

—Editorial: "The Doom of the Black Power," *Frederick Douglass' Paper,* July 27, 1855

Things are often confounded and treated as the same for no better reason than that they seem alike or look alike, and this is done even when in their nature and character they are totally distinct, totally separate, and even opposed to each other. This jumbling up of things is a sort of dust-throwing which is often indulged in by small men who argue for victory rather than for the truth.

—Speech: "The American Constitution and Slavery," March 26, 1860, *Douglass Papers,* ser. I, 3:345

Truth, like the gentle light of Heaven, usually dawns upon more than one mind at the same time, so that there is seldom a discovery which has not more than one to claim the honor of it.

—Speech: "Agriculture and Black Progress," September 18, 1873, *Douglass Papers,* ser. I, 4:378

A lie is only intended to deceive, and when it ceases to fulfill its purpose it is of no value to the liar.

—Speech: "The South Knows Us," May 4, 1879, *Douglass Papers,* ser. I, 4:502

While truth, when contemplated as a totality, is so vast as to transcend man's ability to grasp it in all its fullness and glory, there are, nevertheless, individual truths, sparks from the great All-truth, quite within the range of his mental vision, which, if discovered and obeyed, will light his pathway through the world and make his life successful and happy.

—Speech: "It Moves," November 20, 1883, *Douglass Papers,* ser. I, 5:141

Truth is patient and will finally prevail.

—Correspondence: Douglass to Charles H. Moore, n.d., in Quarles, *Frederick Douglass*, p. 334

Underground Railroad

I have never approved of the very public manner, in which some of our western friends have conducted what they call the "*Under-ground Railroad*," but which, I think, by their open declarations, has been made, most emphatically, the "*Upper*-ground railroad." Its stations are far better known to the slaveholders than to the slaves. . . . Such is my detestation of slavery, that I would keep the merciless slaveholder profoundly ignorant of the means of flight adopted by the slave. He should be left to imagine himself surrounded by myriads of invisible tormentors, ever ready to snatch, from his infernal grasp, his trembling prey.

—Autobiography: *My Bondage and My Freedom*, 1855, p. 185

It is my opinion that thousands would escape from slavery, who now remain, but for the strong cords of affection that bind them to their friends.

—Autobiography: *Narrative*, 1845, p. 74

Usefulness

Usefulness is the price of existence. Do or die, wear out or rust out, bring forth fruit or be cut down, is the law now and always. Men may go often, but they will not go always to an exhausted fountain; they will not long search for substance where they are only rewarded with shadows.

—Speech: "The Anti-Slavery Movement," March 18, 1855, *Douglass Papers*, ser. I, 3:39

Vices

The way of transgression is a bottomless pit, one step in that direction invites the next, and the end is never reached; and it is the same with the path of righteous obedience.

—Autobiography: *Life and Times,* 1881, p. 299

Cowardice

A reputation for cowardice is a constant invitation to abuse and insult. He is always whipt oftenest who is whipt easiest. The coward may be pitied and protected by the magnanimous and brave, but there will always be mean men, and even cowards themselves, who will abuse and insult those whom they can abuse and insult with impunity.

—Speech: "Hope and Despair in These Cowardly Times," May 5, 1861, *Douglass Papers,* ser. I, 3:434

Gossip

It is only necessary to get the rumor well started to have it roll on and increase like a ball in adhesive snow.

—Autobiography: *Life and Times,* 1881, p. 388

Happily, the speculators in human credulity generally reveal the presence of fraud by their elaborate and overdrawn tales of woe and suffering and thus defeat themselves.

—Autobiography: *Life and Times,* 1881, p. 389

[F]alsehood is not easily exposed when it has had an early start in advance of truth.

—Autobiography: *Life and Times,* 1881, p. 442

Greed

Mankind thinks that whatever is prosperous is right. Henry Clay said that what the law has made property, and that 200 years of legislation has made the negro slave property. With a *sang froid* more like that of a demon than a man he added, "It will be asked will not slavery come to an end? Why, that question has been asked fifty years ago, and answered by fifty years of prosperity." . . . Justice is nothing—humanity is nothing—Christianity is nothing—but prosperity is everything.

—Speech: "Texas, Slavery, and American Prosperity," January 2, 1846, *Douglass Papers*, ser. I, 1:123

Among the most numerous and persistent beggars whom I have to encounter in this class are those who come in the character of creditors to demand from me the payment of a debt which I especially owe them for the great services which they or their fathers or grandfathers have rendered to the cause of emancipation.

—Autobiography: *Life and Times*, 1881, p. 389

Indolence

To the pampered love of ease, there is no resting place. What is pleasant to-day, is repulsive tomorrow; what is soft now, is hard at another time; what is sweet in the morning, is bitter in the evening. Neither to the wicked, nor to the idler, is there any solid peace: "*Troubled, like the restless sea.*"

—Autobiography: *My Bondage and My Freedom*, 1855, p. 65

[T]here is not, under the whole heavens, a set of men who cultivate such an intense dread of labor as do the slaveholders. The charge of laziness against the slaves is ever on their lips, and is the standing apology for every species of cruelty and brutality.

—Autobiography: *My Bondage and My Freedom*, 1855, p. 132

That the black man in Slavery shirks labor—aims to do as little as he can, and to do that little in the most slovenly manner—only proves that he is a man. Thackeray says that all men are about as lazy as they can afford to be—and I do not claim that the negro is an exception to this rule. He loves ease and abundance just as other people love ease and abundance. If this is a crime, then all men are criminals, and the negro no more than the rest.

—Speech: "The Black Man's Future in the Southern States," February 5, 1862, *Douglass Papers,* ser. 3, 3:504

Pride

The less character a nation has, the more sensitive do we find it. America is vain, arrogant and jealous, always inquiring of the world, what do you think of me?

—Speech: "Advice to My Canadian Brothers and Sisters," August 3, 1854, *Douglass Papers,* ser. I, 2:530

It is well enough, however, once in a while to remind Americans that they are not alone in this species of self-laudation; that in fact there are many men, reputed wise and good men, living in other parts of the planet, under other forms of government, aristocratic, autocratic, oligarchic, and monarchical, who are just as confident of the good qualities of their government as we are of our own.

—Speech: "Sources of Danger to the Republic," February 7, 1867, *Douglass Papers,* ser. I, 4:150

Intelligence is a great leveler here as elsewhere. It sees plainly the real worth of men and things, and is not easily imposed upon by the dressed up emptiness of human pride.

—Autobiography: *Life and Times,* 1881, p. 322

Virtues

The life of the nation is secure only while the nation is honest, truthful, and virtuous; for upon these conditions depends the life of its life.
  —Speech: "We Are Confronted by a New Administration," April 16, 1885, *Douglass Papers*, ser. I, 5:191

Adaptability
A man is worked upon by what he works on. He may carve out his circumstances, but his circumstances will carve him out as well.
  —Speech: "The Claims of the Negro Ethnologically Considered," July 12, 1854, *Douglass Papers*, ser. I, 2:520

The history of the negro race proves them to be wonderfully adapted to all countries, all climates, and all conditions. Their tenacity of life, their powers of endurance, their malleable toughness, would almost imply especial interposition on their behalf. The ten thousand horrors of slavery, striking hard upon the sensitive soul, have bruised, and battered, and stung, but have not killed. The poor bondman lifts a smiling face above the surface of a sea of agonies, hoping on, hoping ever. His tawny brother, the Indian, dies, under the flashing glance of the Anglo-Saxon. Not so the Negro; civilization cannot kill him. He accepts it—becomes a part of it.
  —Speech: "The Claims of the Negro Ethnologically Considered," July 12, 1854, *Douglass Papers*, ser. I, 2:524

Charity
Anything which looks to assisting the helpless, has my heart and has my hand.
  —Speech: "Trust, the Basis of Charity," January 4, 1853, *Douglass Papers*, ser. I, 2:452

Conviction

Numbers should not be looked to so much as right. The man who is right is a majority. He who has God and conscience on his side, has a majority against the universe. Though he does not represent the present state, he represents the future state. If he does not represent what we are, he represents what we ought to be.

—Speech: "Let All Soil Be Free Soil," August 23, 1852, *Douglass Papers,* ser. I, 2:393

Cooperation

We are one, our cause is one, and we must help each other; if we are to succeed.

—Editorial: *North Star,* December 3, 1847

Courage

The fact is, I never see much use in fighting, unless there is a reasonable probability of whipping somebody.

—Autobiography: *My Bondage and My Freedom,* 1855, p. 167

He should step lightly who sits in judgment upon the weakness of those who pioneer an unpopular cause. Heroic courage is a noble quality but it not always the possession of great minds.

—Speech: "It Moves," November 20, 1883, *Douglass Papers,* ser. I, 5:126

Any man can be brave when there is no danger.

—Speech: "It Moves," November 20, 1883, *Douglass Papers,* ser. I, 5:126

Duty

Duty has been the moving power that has influenced all my actions during all the years of my life. In the past it gave me courage to face the howling mob while contending for the freedom of my people. In the present it gives me courage to endure the abuse of foes, even as it gives me charity for the acts and sayings of those of my people who oppose and assail me. So far as the latter are concerned, I console myself with the knowledge that all of them should be my friends.

—Interview: July 12, 1891, *Douglass Papers,* ser. I, 5:458

Honesty

Honesty is necessary to the faithful compliance with a bargain and just here the South is deficient. Nothing is more true than that the whole moral and social atmosphere of Slavery is unfavorable to the growth of common honesty. The corner-stone of its moral is the maxim that "might makes right." A bargain with a slaveholder will be kept so long as the slaveholder is unable to break it. The right to break comes with the wish and power to break.

—Speech: "We Are in the Midst of a Moral Revolution," May 19, 1854, *Douglass Papers,* ser. I, 2:482

A man's head will not long remain wrong, when his heart is right.

—Autobiography: *Life and Times,* 1881, p. 297

Industry

Man's greatness consists in his ability to do, and the proper application of his powers to things needful to be done, and not in the color of his skin.

—Editorial: "Colored Newspapers," *North Star,* January 7, 1848

Your fathers have lived, died, and have done their work, and have done much of it well. You must live and must die, and you must do your work. You have no right to enjoy a child's share in the labor of your fathers, unless your children are to be blest by your labors. You have no right to wear out and waste the hard-earned fame of your fathers to cover your indolence.

—Speech: "What to the Slave Is the Fourth of July?" July 5, 1852, *Douglass Papers*, ser. I, 2:366

We drink freely of the water at the marble fountain, without thinking for the assessment of the toil and skill displayed in constructing the fountain itself.

—Speech: "Pictures and Progress," December 3, 1861, *Douglass Papers*, ser. I, 3:454

[N]othing valuable shall be obtained without labor and agony.

—Speech: "We Are Not Yet Quite Free," August 3, 1869, *Douglass Papers*, ser. I, 4:221

Work for [money] and save it when you get it. . . . We can work, and the grateful earth yields as readily and as bountifully to the touch of black industry as of white. We can work, and by this means we can retrieve all of our losses.

—Speech: "Agriculture and Black Progress," September 18, 1873, *Douglass Papers*, ser. I, 4:393–94

[A]dvancement is achievable only through patient, enduring, honest, unremitting, and indefatigable work. . . . we may explain success mainly by one word and that word is WORK! WORK!! WORK!!! WORK!!!!

—Speech: "Self-Made Men," March 1893, *Douglass Papers*, ser. I, 5:556, 558

I am certain that there is nothing good, great or desirable which man can possess in this world, that does not come by some kind of labor, physical or mental, moral or spiritual. A man may, at times, get something for nothing, but it will, in his hands, amount to nothing. What is true in the world of matter, is equally true in the world of mind. Without culture there can be no growth; without exertion, no acquisition; without friction, no polish; without labor, no knowledge; without action, no progress and without conflict, no victory. The man who lies down a fool at night, hoping that he will waken wise in the morning, will rise up in the morning as he laid down in the evening.

—Speech: "Self-Made Men," March 1893, *Douglass Papers*, ser. I, 5:555

He who wants hard hands must not, at sight of the first blister, fling away the spade, the rake, the broad axe or the hoe; for the blister is a primary condition to the needed hardness. To abandon work is not only to throw away the means of success, but it is also to part with the ability to work.

—Speech: "Self-Made Men," March 1893, *Douglass Papers*, ser. I, 5:559

They know most of pleasure who seek it least and they least who seek it most. The cushion is soft to him who sits on it but seldom.

—Speech: "Self-Made Men," March 1893, *Douglass Papers*, ser. I, 5:564

Patience
Great bodies move slowly.

—Speech: "Great Bodies Move Slowly," October 25, 1880, *Douglass Papers*, ser. I, 4:584

Perseverance
No, sir, political abolition is not a failure, any more than Christianity is a failure. It is now upward and onward. In my belief the cause will

roll on, and roll till freedom shall be entirely triumphant. Let their motto be, labor and wait.
    —Speech: "We Are in the Midst of a Moral Revolution," May 19, 1854, *Douglass Papers*, ser. I, 2:489–90

A man is never lost while he still earnestly thinks himself worth saving; and as with a man, so with a nation.
    —Speech: "The Final Test of Self-Government," November 13, 1864, *Douglass Papers*, ser. I, 4:36

[N]either slavery, stripes, imprisonment, nor proscription, need extinction self-respect, crush manly ambition, or paralyze effort; that no power outside of himself can prevent a man from sustaining an honorable character and a useful relation to his day and generation. . . .
    —Autobiography: *Life and Times*, 1881, p. 373

Self-Reliance

Our white friends may do much for us, but we must do much for ourselves. Equality and respectability can only be attained by our own exertions. We require respect—not merely sympathy. We have no right to respect, if, being under the hood of oppression, we are not manly enough to rise in our own cause, and do something to elevate ourselves from our degraded position.
    —Speech: "Colonizationist Measures," April 24, 1849, *Douglass Papers*, ser. I, 2:168

All experience has taught that if a man could not stand he must fall, and that if he stood it must be on his own legs.
    —Speech: "Advice to Black Youth," February 1, 1855, *Douglass Papers*, ser. I, 3:3

The general sentiment of mankind is, that a man who will not fight for himself, when he has the means of doing so, is not worth being fought for by others, and this sentiment is just. For a man who does not value freedom for himself will never value it for others, nor put himself to any inconvenience to gain it for other. Such a man the world says, may lay down until he has sense enough to stand up. It is useless and cruel to put a man on his legs, if the next moment his head is to be brought against a curb-stone.

—Speech: "The Significance of Emancipation in the West Indies," August 3, 1857, *Douglass Papers,* ser. I, 3:202

There are three special explanations given as to the cause of success in self-made men. The first attributed to such men superior mental endowments, and assigned this as the true explanation of success. The second made the most of circumstances, favoring opportunities, accidents, chances, &c. The third made industry and application the great secret of success. All had truth in them, and all were capable of being pressed into untruth.

—Speech: "The Trials and Triumphs of Self-Made Men," January 4, 1860, *Douglass Papers,* ser. I, 3:293

The American people have always been anxious to know what they shall do with us. . . . Everybody has asked the question, and they learned to ask it early of the abolitionists: "What shall we do with the negro?" I have had but one answer from the beginning. Do nothing with us! Your doing with us has already played the mischief with us. Do nothing with us! . . . And if the negro cannot stand on his own legs, let him fall also. All I ask is, give him a chance to stand on his own legs! Let him alone! If you see him on his way to school, let him alone,—don't disturb him! If you see him going to the dinner table at a hotel, let him alone! If you see him going to the ballot box, let him alone!—don't disturb him! If you see him going into a workshop, just let him alone,—your interference is doing him positive injury.

—Speech: "What the Black Man Wants?" January 26, 1865, *Douglass Papers*, ser. I, 4:68

My politics in regard to the negro is simply this: Give him fair play and let him alone, but be sure you give him fair play.

—Speech: "Let the Negro Alone," May 11, 1869, *Douglass Papers*, ser. I, 4:202

To ask for help in [the condition of slaves] involved no disgrace. But all is changed now. . . . [The] suppliant, outstretched hand of beggary does not become an American freeman, and does not become us as a class, and we will not consent to be any longer represented in that position.

—Speech: "The Color Question," July 5, 1875, *Douglass Papers*, ser. I, 4:420–21

Properly speaking, there are in the world no such men as self-made men. The term implies an individual independence of the past and present which can never exist.

—Speech: "Self-Made Men," March 1893, *Douglass Papers*, ser. I, 5:549–50

Vigilance
One generation cannot safely rest on the achievements of another, and ought not so to rest.

—Speech: "We Are Confronted by a New Administration," April 16, 1885, *Douglass Papers*, ser. I, 5:176

War

War, stern and terrible war, seems to be the inexorable condition exacted for every considerable addition made to the liberties of mankind. The world moves—let us be thankful for it—but it moves only by fighting every inch of its disputed way. Right and wrong seem alike endowed with fighting qualities—if one does not prevail, the other will and must.

—Speech: "William the Silent," February 8, 1869, *Douglass Papers*, ser. I, 4:187

They are whipped oftenest always who are whipped easiest. The liberties of mankind may be written in ink, but they will gain but little respect until they are written also in blood. It seems that human liberties have been so long entrenched upon, so long trampled upon, that unless the lines of our liberties are marked in blood, tyrants will never cease to overstep them.

—Speech: "William the Silent," February 8, 1869, *Douglass Papers*, ser. I, 4:187–88

Each great nation is steeping to the utmost verge of its power, and employing all of its energies, anticipating all of its resources, tempting bankruptcy and ruin to maintain its army and match the other national armies in numbers, strength, training, skill and efficiency.

—Speech: "My Foreign Travels," December 15, 1887, *Douglass Papers*, ser. I, 5:288

Women
(see also Suffrage)

Equal Rights
Right is of no sex—Truth is of no color—God is the Father of us all, and we are all Brethren.
—Editorial (Masthead): *North Star,* 1847–1851

A discussion of the rights of animals would be regarded with far more complacency by many of what are called the wise and the good of our land, than would be a discussion of the rights of woman.
—Editorial: *North Star,* July 28, 1848

Seize hold of those which are most strongly contested. You have already free access to the paths of literature; Women may write books of poetry, travels, &c. and they will be read with avidity. Let them strike out in some other path where they are not now allowed to go. If there is some kind of business from which they are excluded, let some heroic Woman enter upon that business, as some of these noble Women have entered upon the practice of medicine. Let Woman take her rights, and then she shall be free.
—Speech: "Let Woman Take Her Rights," October 24, 1850, *Douglass Papers,* ser. I, 2:249

The declaration says all men—all men are equal. God made of our blood all nations of men. The United States were included. There is some truth in the slavery of races, some have degenerated, but every race, even the Anglo-Saxon, has been at one time held in slavery. The enslaved Saxon, and Sciavon [Scandian], and German were down then, they are up now. The time will come when the negro will be up. But they say the negro is too ignorant to vote, and they would vote as somebody told them to. Well, if they did, they would do just as you white men do.

—Speech: "Govern with Magnanimity and Courage," September 6, 1866, *Douglass Papers*, ser. I, 4:144

All good causes are mutually helpful. The benefits accruing from this movement for the equal rights of woman are not confined or limited to woman only. They will be shared by every effort to promote the progress and welfare of mankind everywhere and in all ages.

—Speech: "Give Women Fair Play," March 31, 1888, *Douglass Papers*, ser. I, 5:355

Moral Sense

[L]ong experience has confirmed me in the opinion that, however cold and indifferent to human suffering, however dead and stone-like, the heart of man may, under the influence of sordid avarice, become, the heart of woman is ever warm, tenderly alive, and throbs in deepest sympathy with the sorrows and sufferings of every class, colour, and clime, over the globe. She is the last to inflict injury and the first to repair it. If she is ever found in the ranks of the enemies of freedom, she is there at the bidding of man, and in open disobedience to her own noble nature.

—Speech: "Charges and Defense of the Free Church," March 10, 1846, *Douglass Papers*, ser. I, 1:171–72

Natural Abilities

[A] woman should have every honorable motive to exertion which is enjoyed by man, to the full extent of her capacities and endowments. The case is too plain for argument. Nature has given woman the same powers, and subjected her to the same earth, breathes the same air, subsists on the same food, physical, moral, mental and spiritual. She has, therefore, an equal right with man, in all efforts to obtain and maintain a perfect existence.

—Speech: "Speech at the 1848 Women's Rights Convention at Seneca Falls," in Philip S. Foner, *Frederick Douglass on Women's Rights* (Westport, Conn.: Greenwood Press, 1976), 58

NOTE ON EDITORIAL METHOD

The editors of this collection are also staff members of the Frederick Douglass Papers, founded in 1973. They have a long history of participation in the systematic effort—funded by the National Historical Publications and Records Commission, the National Endowment for the Humanities, and a number of generous private foundations—to locate and publish accurate texts of Douglass's spoken and written words. Although this current volume is not part of that ongoing project, it draws heavily on the scrupulous textual editing standards of the Douglass Papers for selecting, reproducing, and citing Douglass quotations.

Quotation Selection

The principal criteria governing the editors' decisions about which quotations by Douglass to select for reproduction are amply discussed in the preface to this collection. One other key decision that the editors made for this volume was not to include any quotation that could not be firmly attributed to Douglass's authorship. In their research, the editors discovered dozens of quotations in print or on the Internet that could not be conclusively traced back to a particular speech or writing by Douglass or, worse, were actually the product of another speaker or writer. The body of Douglass's verifiable statements is so vast and their quality is so rich that the editors decided that there was no need to include any questionable item in this collection.

The editors have categorized the Douglass quotations according to the most significant idea of the statement. They sometimes have provided subcategories in the interest of further clarification. Because Douglass sometimes addressed the same topic repeatedly over more than a half century of public life, the editors have chosen to arrange their presentation chronologically within each category or subcategory to illustrate the evolution of his thinking.

Textual Methodology

As experienced textual editors, the team preparing this volume was used to reproducing the texts of Douglass's words as close as possible to how he spoke or wrote them, even if that required the reproduction of misspelled or inaccurate words or names. This form of critical editing also necessitated the reproduction of Douglass's spoken statements in their entirety, including all the digressions and interruptions that accompany any speech or interview. In considering the needs of the intended readership for *In the Words of Frederick Douglass*, the editors decided that it would be beneficial to silently correct such errors and to modernize obscure spelling, missing capitalization, or distracting punctuation. Where lengthy or digressive statements have been extracted for this collection, the editors have inserted ellipses to indicate where there are intentional omissions. Scholars in need of exact texts are guided by notes to either the published texts of the Frederick Douglass Papers or the original sources of the quotation, whichever is most appropriate.

Sources for Quotations

There are many sources for Frederick Douglass's quotations, but the principal categories are his speeches, his correspondence, his journalistic writing, and his autobiographies.

Speeches. The Frederick Douglass Papers has documented literally thousands of Douglass's speeches, debates, and interviews from the years 1842 to his death in 1895. The texts of many of those Douglass's addresses have not survived, but a systematic search uncovered a large number of his oral statements. In some cases, Douglass's notes or full-length manuscripts for his speeches and lectures have survived in his papers now preserved by the Library of Congress. Many more texts were recovered from the newspapers of the era, which frequently reported on Douglass's public appearances on behalf of many different causes. Finally, Douglass himself published many of what he regarded as his most significant addresses in his newspapers, separate pamphlets, and even his autobiographies. When we have extracted quotations from one of these speeches, we have accepted the determination made by the Douglass Papers of the best of sometimes several available sources for the text of that oral statement. That source is listed after the text of the quotation in a note supplying the title of the address, the date of its delivery, and the location of the full document in the Douglass Papers series. Readers interested in inspecting the actual document can obtain that information by consulting the Douglass Papers.

Correspondence. Douglass corresponded tens of thousands of times with his contemporaries. Thanks to his international reputation as a reformer, several thousand of his letters, dating back to only a few years after he gained his freedom, can be found in numerous library manuscript collections, government archives, and private holdings in the United States and many other nations. The Douglass Papers has collected copies of all these letters and is in the process of publishing the most historically significant of them. When possible, the editors of this volume have relied on the Douglass Papers for the texts of quotations originally appearing in Douglass's letters. In those cases, the source appears in a note following the quotation, supplying the name of the other correspondent, the date of the letter, and the location of the document in the Douglass Papers. Other times, the editors have had to rely on contemporary newspapers or other published collections of Douglass documents for the text of quotations from Douglass letters. In those cases, the name of the correspondent and date of the letter are again supplied along with a brief description of that alternative source, with full publication information supplied in our bibliography.

Editorials/Essays. Douglass provided incisive commentary on public affairs during his lifetime as editor of four different periodicals and as a sought-after contributing author to many other periodicals. Because of a devastating 1872 fire at Douglass's home in Rochester, New York, his own personal archive of bound copies of his three antislavery newspapers, the *North Star,* the *Frederick Douglass' Paper,* and the *Douglass' Monthly,* all originally published in that city, were destroyed. Efforts by the Douglass Papers staff resulted in the recovery of copies of more than 80 percent of those issues now found in libraries and repositories across the United States. More than 1,200 of Douglass's own editorials in these three papers as well as his *New National Era,* published in Washington, D.C., in the 1870s, have survived. A careful search of contemporary periodicals revealed more than thirty additional articles written by Douglass for other newspapers and magazines. The Douglass Papers envisions publishing a two-volume selected collection of those journalistic works. The editors of this volume have studied that large collection to locate quotations that represent Douglass's published commentary on a diverse range of issues. For each quotation in this category, a source note gives the title of the editorial or article, the name of the newspaper or magazine, and the date that the item was originally published.

Autobiographies. Frederick Douglass was practically unique in having composed and published three separate autobiographies during his lifetime. The first, *Narrative of the Life of Frederick Douglass, an American Slave,* was written in 1845 and published by his Boston abolitionist associates. Douglass wrote this book to answer critics who doubted that his claim to be a runaway slave. In his *Narrative,* Douglass not only provided the personal details to prove his enslaved past but authored a brilliant indictment of human bondage. This extremely well-written autobiography became not only a widely circulated abolitionist weapon but also a significant piece of American literary history, continuously in print down to today. Only ten years after *Narrative,* in 1855, Douglass wrote and published his second autobiography, *My Bondage and My Freedom.* More than double the length of its predecessor, *My Bondage and My Freedom* was also intended as an abolitionist propaganda tool. It provided many more details about the inhumane treatment that Douglass had observed as well as personally endured during his youth as a Maryland slave. This book is noteworthy because it also gives an account of Douglass's early experiences in the North, first as a laborer in New Bedford, Massachusetts, and then as a paid antislavery lecturer. Douglass not only provided interesting details on the early history of the abolitionist movement but documented the pervasive racism he encountered throughout antebellum northern society. In 1881, Douglass published his third autobiography, the *Life and Times of Frederick Douglass.* This work retells Douglass's life as a slave and as an abolitionist and then proceeds to recount his life as a Civil War army recruiter, a holder of important postwar governmental offices, a Republican Party political campaigner, and a leading spokesperson for the rights of the freed slaves. In 1892, Douglass expanded *Life and Times* by adding details of his later public services, especially his ambassadorship to the Caribbean republic of Haiti, and of his extensive tour of Europe and Egypt. These three autobiographies contain numerous statements by Douglass not only on his life experiences but on all aspects of nineteenth-century government, culture, and race relations. The Douglass Papers has reproduced each of these autobiographies in modern editions that follow the highest standards of critical editing to avoid the corruptions in language that appear in many of the reprinted versions of these three works. When this current collection extracts a quotation from one of the autobiographies, the source is identified in a note by a short title for the book, followed by the page number on which the passage appears in the Douglass Papers edition.

SELECTED BIBLIOGRAPHY

Original Documents by Frederick Douglass

Blassingame, John W., and John R. McKivigan, eds. *The Frederick Douglass Papers*. Series 1: *Speeches, Debates, and Interviews*. 5 vols. New Haven: Yale University Press, 1979–1992.

——, eds. *The Frederick Douglass Papers*. Series 2: *Autobiographical Writings*. 3 vols. New Haven: Yale University Press, 1999–2011.

Foner, Philip S., ed. *Frederick Douglass on Women's Rights*. Westport, Conn.: Greenwood Press, 1976.

——, ed. *Life and Writings of Frederick Douglass*. 5 vols. New York: International Publishers, 1950–75.

McCurdy, Michael, ed. *Escape from Slavery: The Boyhood of Frederick Douglass in His Own Words*. New York: Alfred A. Knopf, 1994.

McKivigan, John R., ed. *The Frederick Douglass Papers*. Series 3: *Correspondence*. New Haven: Yale University Press, 2009.

Meltzer, Milton, ed. *Frederick Douglass, in His Own Words*. San Diego, Calif.: Harcourt Brace, 1995.

Biographies and Studies of Frederick Douglass

Andrews, William, ed. *The Oxford Frederick Douglass Reader*. New York: Oxford University Press, 1996.

Bennett, Evelyn. *Frederick Douglass and the War against Slavery*. Brookfield, Conn.: The Millbrook Press, 1993.

Blight, David W. *Frederick Douglass's Civil War: Keeping the Faith in Jubilee.* Baton Rouge: Louisiana State University Press, 1989.

Dietrich, Maria. *Love across Color Lines: Ottilie Asking & Frederick Douglass.* New York: Hill and Wang, 1999.

Foner, Philip S. *Frederick Douglass.* New York: Citadel Press, 1950.

Gregory, James M. *Frederick Douglass, the Orator.* [1893.] Reprint. New York: Apollo Editions, 1971.

Huggins, Nathan Irvin. *Slave and Citizen: The Life of Frederick Douglass.* Edited by Oscar Handlin. Boston: Little, Brown, 1980.

Keenan, Sheila. *Frederick Douglass: Portrait of a Freedom Fighter.* New York: Scholastic, 1995.

Larson, Bill, and Frank Kirkland, eds. *Frederick Douglass: A Critical Reader.* New York: Wiley-Blackwell, 1999.

Levine, Robert S. *Martin Delany, Frederick Douglass, and the Politics of Representative Identity.* Chapel Hill: University of North Carolina Press, 1997.

Martin, Waldo E., Jr. *The Mind of Frederick Douglass.* Chapel Hill: University of North Carolina Press, 1984.

McFeely, William S. *Frederick Douglass.* New York: W. W. Norton, 1991.

McKissack, Patricia, and Fredrick McKissack. *Frederick Douglass: The Black Lion.* Chicago: Children's Press, 1987.

Myers, Peter C. *Frederick Douglass: Race and the Rebirth of American Liberalism.* Lawrence: University of Kansas Press, 2008.

Miller, Douglass T. *Frederick Douglass and the Fight for Freedom.* New York: Facts on File, 1988.

Oakes, James. *The Radical and the Republican: Frederick Douglass, Abraham Lincoln, and the Triumph of Antislavery Politics.* New York: W. W. Norton, 2007.

Preston, Dickson J. *Young Frederick Douglass: The Maryland Years.* Baltimore: Johns Hopkins University Press, 1980.

Quarles, Benjamin. *Frederick Douglass.* 1948; New York: Da Capo, 1997.

Rice, Allan J., and Martin Crawford. *Liberating Sojourn: Frederick Douglass & Transatlantic Reform.* Athens: University of Georgia Press, 1999.

Russell, Sharman Apt. *Frederick Douglass.* New York: Chelsea House, 1988.

Stauffer, John. *Giants: The Parallel Lives of Frederick Douglass and Abraham Lincoln.* New York: Twelve Publishers, 2009.

Voss, Frederick S. *Majestic in His Wrath: A Pictorial Life of Frederick Douglass.* Washington, D.C.: Smithsonian Institution Press, 1995.

Washington, Booker T. *Frederick Douglass.* Philadelphia: George W. Jacobs & Company, 1906.

General Histories of the Abolitionist and Early Civil Rights Movements

Aptheker, Herbert. *Abolitionism: A Revolutionary Movement.* Boston: Twayne, 1989.

Blight, David W. *Race and Reunion: The Civil War in American Memory.* Cambridge, Mass.: Belknap Press of Harvard University, 2002.

Dillon, Merton L. *Slavery Attacked: Southern Slaves and Their Allies, 1619–1865.* Baton Rouge: Louisiana State University Press, 1990.

Fields, Barbara Jeanne. *Slavery and Freedom in the Middle Ground: Maryland in the Nineteenth Century.* New York: Oxford University Press, 1986.

Friedman, Lawrence J. *Gregarious Saints: Self and Community in American Abolitionism, 1830–1870.* New York: Cambridge University Press, 1983.

Hinks, Peter P. *To Awaken My Afflicted Brethren: David Walker and the Problem of Antebellum Slave Resistance.* University Park: Pennsylvania State University Press, 1997.

Levine, Lawrence. *Black Culture and Black Consciousness: Afro-American Folk Thought from Slavery to Freedom.* New York: Oxford University Press, 1977.

Litwack, Leon F. *Trouble in Mind: Southern Blacks in the Age of Jim Crow.* New York: Vintage, 1999.

McPherson, James M. *The Abolitionist Legacy: From Reconstruction to the NAACP.* Princeton: Princeton University Press, 1975.

Moses, Wilson J. *The Golden Age of Black Nationalism, 1850–1925.* Hamden, Conn.: Archon Books, 1978.

Painter, Nell Irvin. *Exodusters: Black Migration to Kansas after Reconstruction.* New York: Knopf, 1976.

Pease, Jane H., and William H. Pease. *They Who Would Be Free: Blacks' Search for Freedom, 1830–1861.* New York: Athenaeum, 1974.

Stauffer, John. *The Black Hearts of Men: Radical Abolitionists and the Transformation of Race.* Cambridge, Mass.: Harvard University Press, 2002.

Stewart, James Brewer. *Holy Warriors: The Abolitionists and American Slavery.* [1976.] 2d ed. New York: Hill and Wang, 1997.

Williamson, Joel. *The Crucible of Race: Black/White Relations in the American South since Emancipation.* New York: Oxford University Press, 1984.

Wintz, Cary D. *African American Political Thought 1890–1930: Washington, Dubois, Garvey, and Randolph.* Armonk, N.Y.: M. E. Sharpe, 1996.

Woodward, C. Vann. *The Strange Career of Jim Crow.* 3rd rev. ed. New York: Oxford University Press, 1974.

INDEX